Sinai and the Red Sea

Wolfgang and Rosel Jahn

Sinai and the Red Sea

Across the Land of the Bedouin
to the Gulf of Aqaba

The American University in Cairo Press

First published in Germany as *Sinai und Rotes Meer:*
Durch das Land der Bedouinen bis zum Golf von Akaba.
Copyright © 1994 by Chr. Belser AG für Verlagsgeschäfte & Co. KG,
Stuttgart und Zürich

Dar el Kutub No. 11768/96
ISBN 977 424 419 2

Printed in Italy

Contents

Impressions

**From the "Desert of Confusion" over Mount Sinai
to the Magic Gardens of the Red Sea**

Sinai – the word exudes fascination and conjures associations: land of Exodus and Revelation, pharaohs' land of turquoise and copper, pilgrimage route of devout Muslims, sanctuary of Christian monks, military road and trade route of ancient Egypt and Rome, holy land of three religions, and theater of modern tank battles. For a desert, Sinai is a land surprisingly rich in history. Located between the continents of Africa and Asia, the peninsula is an enormous triangular wedge, forming both a dividing desert and a connecting land bridge. In ancient times the Sinai desert acted as a buffer between the Nile Valley and the Near Eastern empires, allowing ancient Egypt to flourish as a great power almost undisturbed. But the desert is not insuperable and there has been interplay between Palestine and Egypt throughout history. Travelers have come to Sinai since early times, when a journey here was arduous. The first known Sinai tourist was the Spanish nun Aetheria, who visited the Burning Bush and prayed on Mount Sinai at the end of the fourth century. Modern journeys of discovery began in 1762 with the Danish 'Arabia Felix' expedition.

Regardless of the direction of approach, the traveler to Sinai is immediately struck by a jagged, inhospitable, but also impressive landscape with dramatic contrasts. Little by little one perceives that it is exactly these apparently incompatible contrasts that constitute the fascination of Sinai. Some find the desert landscape and the Red Sea unfriendly, even dangerous and frightening. The dusty, dry, shimmering air, the leaden, yellow-gray sky, the livid and glaring sun blazing its unbearably harsh light on the stark landscape, the gusting wind that makes the heat more palpable-all these elements are overwhelming and make the apparently endless desert seem even more oppressive. And it all turns to torture when a sandstorm rages. The body is covered with sweat and dust. Sand gets into mouth and nose, a dull, gnawing headache dazes, and persistent flies attack.

Another phenomenon also threatens in the desert. The dry valleys, the wadis, may be so dessicated that for years and sometimes decades hardly a plant survives. Everything is shriveled or dead. Then suddenly, and with elemental force, water cascades through the wadis, which turn from one moment to the next into torrential mountain streams. One might not even notice the storm that has opened its floodgates a few kilometers away, and is flushing away cars and even recently-built roads. After seeing the traces of such natural disasters with our own eyes, we understand the meaning of the old saying that more people drown than die of thirst in the desert.

But – and herein lies the peculiarity of Sinai-conditions change rapidly and unexpectedly. The dusty, blazing heat of midday is followed by the cool, wonderfully clear night. On the highest mountains it can even snow in winter. Where powerful floods have recently brought death and devastation, a green carpet with red, yellow, blue, violet, and white flowers spreads itself over pure sand, and in astonishment we stand before the wonder of the blooming desert. (**Fig. pages 34–35**) The landscape also changes drastically: wasted gravel fields suddenly turn into a charming dune landscape. And around a bend, a small wadi ends in a wild and deeply-fissured gorge. In the steep rock cliffs are hidden colored deposits that seem more human art than natural formations. In the middle of the broadest loneliness of the mountains, the greatest monument of human culture – St. Catherine's Monastery (**Fig. page 88–89**) – is located. (The external façade of the monastery resembles a stark fortress, but the interior is lavishly decorated with Byzantine art.) At the Gulf of Aqaba, fissured, reddish granite mountains descend from a height of 2000 meters into the deep blue water of the Red Sea. At a glance, the Red Sea seems to be a desert of water, as lifeless as the landscape around it. Nothing could be further from the truth. A look beneath the water's surface reveals the fantastic world of the coral reef: an underwater landscape replete with colors and forms that overflow with life.

The astonishing contrasts of Sinai continually amaze us. Once, we hiked from the foot of Gabal Katrin to Gabal Umm Shomar, the second-highest mountain of the central massif of southern Sinai. The sharp ridges and towers of the heavily eroded granite rose steeply to the azure sky, and we felt as if we were in the wildest and loneliest sea of rocks imaginable. We then happened upon a steep valley and were astounded at what lay before us: under the green foliage of tall palm trees overloaded with amber-colored dates, red pomegranates shone like rubies and ripe oranges hung from deep green branches. There were almond and mulberry trees, and fresh, clear water flowed in little ditches through this garden surrounded by stone walls. Farther on, on a slope, we discovered two small houses and the ruins of a small church, still adorned with a wooden cross. In the middle of the inhospitable stony desert, we stood before this Eden-like garden.

Whoever makes their way from the north through the terrible "Desert of Confusion" across the granite massif of Mount Sinai (Gabal Musa) to the magic gardens of the Red Sea will experience a variety of nature completely unexpected in the midst of such a barren landscape. The range of geological features alone creates new views and impressions. As the changing light of day and season plays fantastically upon the mountains, dunes, acacias, wadis, rocks, gorges, and plains, the same panorama is dramatically altered.

Light plays a very important role in Sinai. Anybody who has enjoyed the sunrise on top of Mount Sinai or another lonely peak has experienced its magic. In such a steep and sublime wilderness, the way light changes the face of this expanse touches people and is certainly partly responsible for the great religious impulses that have had their origin in Sinai. It is easy to understand why people of so many varied backgrounds become enchanted by this landscape and always wish to return, and why some wish to leave everything behind and remain in Sinai forever.

Geology and Geography

A Desert in the Water

The ancient Mesopotamian moon-god Sin probably gave his name to the land bridge between Africa and Asia, the peninsula that is washed by the Mediterranean Sea in the north and by the Red Sea in the south. Sin, who was equated with the moon god Thoth by the ancient Egyptians, is said still to be honored in Sinai. This is easy to believe when one sees a full moon over the desert.

The derivation of the name of the Red Sea is more problematic. In the bright midday sun, the water displays a spectrum of blues only the sea can produce. It is the bluest sea we know. Almost a dozen explanations for the name have been given, but all remain speculations. We have found our own explanation: on some winter evenings, immediately after sunset, the Red Sea is ablaze in an orgy of reds. If only for a few minutes, the sky glows in a display of orange-red fireworks, and colors ranging from red to deep violet are reflected on the water.

Geologically, Sinai is a very young formation of the earth's crust. In the late Eocene era, about forty million years ago, enormous fault movements formed the great African Rift Valley and the Red Sea with its two gulfs, and the peninsula became separated from the Arabo-Nubian massif. A nearly isosceles triangle of land was formed 200 kilometers west to east and 380 kilometers north to south, with a total area of 61,000 square kilometers. Geologically and geographically, Sinai does not end at its present political border but includes the Negev Desert of Israel. The Dead Sea is also a formation of the rift system.

A drive across Sinai is a journey through the geological history of the peninsula. One of the characteristics of this unique landscape is that it reveals in a relatively small area its geological history from one billion years ago to the present. In the course of this journey, one experiences not only a variety of forms and colors but also the changing structure of the landscape, which demonstrates the earth's creative strength and contributes to Sinai's attraction. The peninsula is a tilted plate in the earth's crust that slopes downward in the north and is uplifted in the south. Because of this, one can see the geological present in the area of the Mediterranean coast, where even today sediments are deposited on the sloping shore, while erosion in the south has uncovered ancient and originally low-lying formations of rocks. The geographical situation of Sinai in the Afro-Asian desert zone, where arid-climate plants grow very sparsely, leads to a threadbare soil that is easily subjected to such widespread erosion.

For thousands of years, north and northwest winds have driven sand from the Sahara that has been brought down to the sea in enormous quantities by the Nile. Thus was formed the lovely dune belt that extends along the coast, twenty to fifty kilometers wide. Only parts of the dunes are moving, and the plentiful winter rains bring enough water to allow agriculture on these soft, sandy slopes. The scenes of Bedouin men digging furrows with a primitive plow (**Fig. pages 102–3**) followed by veiled women sowing melon seeds are almost biblical. Not surprisingly, the northern coastal region of Sinai is the part of the peninsula that has water, and the majority of Sinai inhabitants, mainly settled Bedouin, live there. The Bedouin community has also been augmented by many immigrants from Egypt who moved to Sinai after it was liberated from Israeli occupation in 1982.

Palm oases are scattered among these northern dunes. Also situated here is the north's main city, al-Arish, which is surrounded by magnificent palm groves. Located on the Via Maris between Egypt and Palestine, al-Arish has a long history as a trading and caravan center, although today the historical remains are few. Al-Arish now serves as a tourist center and the administrative capital of North Sinai.

The beautiful palm beaches on the Mediterranean coast are not always clean, and some have been disfigured by building projects. Moreover, there is a great military presence in the area, and visitors are not allowed on the beaches after sunset. Winter rains coming from the Mediterranean feed numerous springs and wells, even deep in the interior. The Ain al-Gedeirat spring, at the village of Quseima near the Israeli border, is one of the most abundant in Sinai and well worth seeing. A trip to this spring requires permission from the authorities in al-Arish. This can be a frustrating introduction to the local bureaucracy and demands patience and persuasiveness.

Plant growth and water do not necessarily keep dunes stable. The relentless shift of dunes is caused by strong winds, and sands driven by the northwest winds bury streets, oases, villages, and springs. Human countermeasures can slow this natural process but can never hope to stop it. Only the waterflows of Wadi al-Arish repeatedly break through the dune belt.

Strong marine currents have also built up sandbanks that have cut off Lake Bardawil (Sabkhat al-Bardawil). Due to rapid evaporation, the lake has a high salinity and so is used not only used for fishing but also for salt production. Bible researchers continue to discuss whether the 'Reed Sea,' across which the Israelites escaped under the leadership of Moses and where the Pharaoh's troops were drowned, is located here. The lake is named after the Crusader king Baldwin (Arabic: Bardawil), who was killed here at the beginning of the twelfth century in one of the wars between Crusaders and Egyptian Muslims.

The area northeast of the Suez Canal is a geologically distinct region. Geographically, it belongs to Sinai, but it is actually part of the Nile Delta with its silt deposits. Aerial pictures show the course of a buried arm of the Nile that flowed into the sea near the ancient city of Pelusium. Nile mud has even been found during excavations of the city itself. Standing in the midst of these ruins, it is hard to imagine that this city was once a flourishing Mediterranean harbor. The deposits of this old arm of the Nile were so overwhelming that today remnants of the city wall and stumps of pillars jut out of the Nile mud many kilometers from the shore. Pelusium is historically important as the scene of the murder of Pompey, whom the Roman Senate had appointed guardian of the children of Ptolemy XII. Caesar used the murder of Pompey as an opportunity to seize final power over Egypt.

To the south of the dune belt lies the extensive Tih Plateau, interrupted only by the ridges (**Fig. pages 22–23**) of Gabal Maghara, Gabal Halal, and Gabal Yi'allaq.

To the hurried traveler crossing this truly deserted area, the Tih Plateau is the most desolate part of Sinai, covering three-quarters of its total area. In the Bible, this part of the peninsula was described as a "great and terrible wilderness" (Deut. 1:19). Nevertheless, even here one can experience in great solitude the changing landscape caused by the variations in light of the broad sky. Away from the road, there are said to be hidden natural splendors that can be reached with difficulty by desert tracks. Today, minefields, dangerous war debris, and extensive prohibited areas make a trip to these secluded places all but impossible.

The Tih Plateau consists partly of dazzling white limestone deposited in the Eocene period. Following this, the soft limestone and chalk deposits were eroded and formed slopes and hollows that are sometimes covered with flint over large areas. This flint was an invaluable material for tool production in the Stone Age. Only a few hundred meters higher, mountain ranges with no distinctive peaks rise above the plain. They consist of hard limestones with Jurassic strata. Coal finds on Gabal Maghara date from the middle Jurassic period.

This geological cross-section (after Edouard Lambelet) shows the inclined Sinai slab that sinks toward the Mediterranean in the north (left) and rises in the south (right). The strata that are sedimented over the crystalline basement complex are completely preserved in the north while toward the south these strata are increasingly eroded so that finally in the southern central massif (Mount Sinai) the basement complex appears. The igneous dikes in the area of Mount Sinai point to a volcanic past for the basement complex.

Geological Cross-Section of the Sinai Peninsula

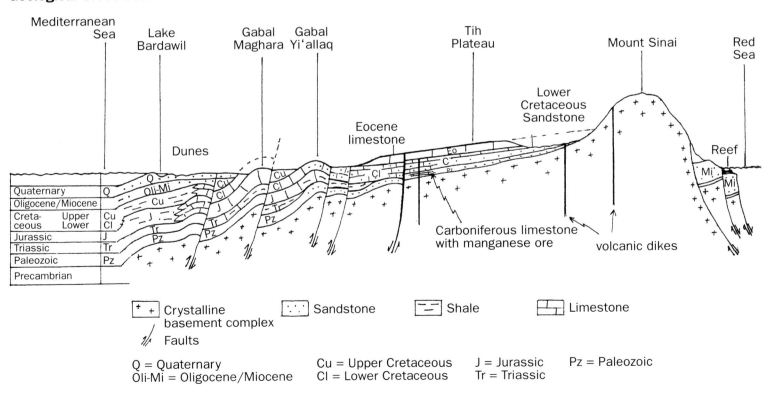

Quaternary	Q
Oligocene/Miocene	
Creta-ceous Upper	Cu
Lower	Cl
Jurassic	J
Triassic	Tr
Paleozoic	Pz
Precambrian	

Q = Quaternary
Oli-Mi = Oligocene/Miocene
Cu = Upper Cretaceous
Cl = Lower Cretaceous
J = Jurassic
Tr = Triassic
Pz = Paleozoic

The powerful Wadi al-Arish, with its numerous side-valleys, has carved through the elevated land and drains the Tih Plateau in the south. Like branches of a tree, the valleys meet in the main wadi creating a 'trunk' that heads northward to the Mediterranean coast. It is amazing how such an extended valley system could emerge from this desert land, and in fact it is a fossil drainage system from the rainy Ice Age.

Travelers who use the highway from the Suez Canal tunnel to Taba will cross these wadis repeatedly. Especially fascinating are the valley crossings in the area around Nakhl. Important springs, which have always determined the routes of travel, are located at the old caravan stations of Nakhl, Bir Hasana, Bir Gafgafa, Bir Rod Salim, and Bir al-Thamada.

The Tih plateau gradually ascends from north to south and pushes on a semicircular front into southern Sinai. (**Map page 16**) This is the least developed part of Sinai and is best crossed by camel. Old pilgrim paths like the Darb al-Hagg and the Darb al-Shawi cross the desert from west to east and still make up parts of the modern roads leading from the Canal tunnel over the Mitla Pass, through Nakhl and al-Thamad, to the steep descent to Eilat. Not far from the Mitla Pass, Salah al-Din, Ayyubid sultan of Egypt, built the fortress of Qal'at al-Gundi on an imposing, deeply-fissured limestone mountain (**Fig. page 92**). This fortress protected the pilgrims who came from Wadi Sidr to meet the pilgrimage routes to the east.

The Tih Plateau, bounded on the southwest by the Gabal al-Tih and on the southeast by the Gabal al-Igma, has recently been designated by geologists the Gabal al-Tih – Igma-Plateau. At the southern edge of the plateau it becomes clear that what was apparently a high plateau is in reality a slowly rising slope which suddenly ends at Gabal al-Tih or Gabal al-Igma, where it drops straight down for up to 700 meters and offers a splendid view toward the south. After a narrow plain covered with yellow-red sand come mountains consisting of stratified sandstone. On the tilted Sinai slab, these strata sink under the chalk layers of the Tih fault. The age of these fossil rocks is difficult to determine; all that is certain is that they date from a very long deposition period of approximately 350 million years (from the Carboniferous to the Cretaceous periods).

Behind the sandstone elevations in the south, the jagged peaks of the Sinai central massif are clearly visible under the bright blue sky. Spontaneously the eye tries to make out the peaks of Mount Sinai and Gabal Katrin. The view reveals the oldest history of the earth, for erosion has exposed the roots of the mountains, Precambrian rocks that rose as melted magma from the bowels of the earth 1,000 million years ago.

Before we turn finally to the dramatic southern part of Sinai, let us return to the Tih fault and its border areas. The steep face is so precipitous that it is a genuine, nearly insurmountable barrier. Only a few small serpentine paths make descent possible. Here the thick sequence of stratified chalk is visible, under which the older, southerly-exposed sandstone disappears. This sandstone belt dividing northern Sinai from the high central massif of southern Sinai has been important to humans for ages. In the western part are turquoise, malachite, and copper deposits that were mined by ancient Egyptians. The most famous turquoise finds are at Serabit al-Khadim and the caves of Maghara. Important copper mines existed, for example, near Bir Nasib and in Wadi Kharrig. Yet the pharaohs were not the first to exploit these mines. Their precursors date almost as far back as the Neolithic Age. Even today, turquoise is occasionally found in the Sinai, but it is not much prized, as with time it can fade.

The regions west of the Tih Plateau on the Gulf of Suez are of special geological interest. This later extension of the Red Sea has its origin in the Carboniferous period, but it became only a relatively unimportant sidearm when the great African Rift Valley system developed. Especially interesting are geological processes that show that the development of the faults is not yet finished. The severe earthquake that shook Cairo in late 1992 arose from an obviously still young fault zone extending from the Gulf of Suez under Cairo to Alexandria. The warm springs at Uyun Musa ('Springs of Moses') and Hammam al-Fara'un ('Pharaoh's Bath') north of Abu Zenima, whose waters reach 70° centigrade, are evidence of deep earth movements. According to Bedouin legends, the pharaoh was killed here when he perse-cuted the Israelites during their Exodus from Egypt. Allegedly, his cursed soul lives on in the warm steam of a nearby cave. But this legend does not prevent old Bedouin from resting for hours in the cave after bathing in the hot sulfur springs by the shore to relieve their rheumatic pains. Just a few kilometers south of Hammam al-Fara'un, before the road near Abu Zenima leaves the mountains, there is another wonderful geological sight at the Tayiba Oasis. As the great African Rift Valley developed, hot magma came up and formed a black basalt band in the layers of white chalk. Due to the intense heat, the underlying layers were baked by the liquid rock and turn-ed red. As a result, an unusually colored mountain face forms the backdrop for a green oasis today. A little farther back, strongly inclined strata are visible, indicating a main fault of the Gulf of Suez.

Various raw materials of this region are of economic importance: oil is extracted in the Gulf of Suez, primarily in the region of Abu Rudeis. North of Hammam al-Faraun, near Abu Malaab, there is a US-sponsored project to mine Miocene plaster for building materials or for neutralizing salty soil. South of Abu Zenima are the access roads that lead east to the local man-ganese mines, centered at Umm Bugma, not far from Serabit al-Khadim. Manganese, which is used in steel production, was not mined by ancient Egyptians. Since the deposits are not very productive, many mines have had to be closed. The manganese produced nowadays is shipped from the little harbour at Abu Zenima.

The sandstone belt with its mountains molded by water, wind, heat, and cold and its deeply washed and wild romantic gorges, in parts fan-tastically colored, belongs to South Sinai and is one of the most inter-esting parts of the peninsula. The names Colored Canyon and Rainbow Canyon (**Fig. page 30**) reflect the fact that sedimentation and erosion have created real works of art near Nuweiba. The picturesque oasis of Ain Hudra and the Wadi Arada (**Fig. pages 24 & 26**) are well-known tou-rist destinations, where the occasional torrents of water have worn away the sandstone, forming nearly vertical chimney-like pillars. Around every curve and in every corner new and fantastic natural formations wait to be discovered.

The road to St. Catherine's Monastery crosses this area from west to east, running sometimes through sandstone, sometimes through the crystal-line basement complex. South of Abu Rudeis the road leaves the Gulf of Suez and leads first through Wadi Feiran and later through Wadi al-Sheikh to the Watia Pass, from where St. Catherine's Monastery is reached by a small side road. The main road continues east to the Gulf of Aqaba. From a scenic and geological point of view, this Sinai crossing is one of the most varied and beautiful routes of all. It passes through Pliocene and Miocene sediments, Cretaceous chalk, and Permian-Triassic sandstone. In Wadi Feiran gneiss, the oldest of the rocks of Sinai, appears for the first time. Shortly thereafter, the jagged granite peaks of Gabal Serban appear, the most impressive mountain mass of Sinai.

In the Feiran Oasis and further to the east, bright yellow deposits appear in front of cliffs of granite and gneiss. These deposits are probably the sediments of a chain of lakes that were formed before Wadi Feiran was washed out and became a valley. In Wadi al-Sheikh especially, the gneiss is penetrated by green, red, and black porphyric bands, volcanic dikes that rose in fissures of the older stone caused by movements in the earth's crust or earthquakes; through parallel crevices and intersections they have produced remarkable patterns in the craggy landscape. These dikes probably did not originally reach the surface but were exposed much later through erosion. Where these volcanic rocks are stronger than the surrounding granite, they form raised ridges. Softer rocks give way sooner to erosion and form channels.

Soon after passing through the rock defile of al-Buayb ('little gate') and through the tamarisk oasis of al-Tarfet, the central massif of younger, red granite can be seen towering upward. A little later comes the narrow entrance to the Watia Pass. (Here, on the right, the sight of a small white Byzantine chapel in the midst of this stony red wilderness surprises the traveler.) In the vicinity of Mount Sinai and Gabal Katrin (at 2,642 meters the highest peak of Sinai), younger and older rock types are found in abundance. In addition to the younger and stronger red granite, there is the older, Precambrian gray to pink granite, which weathers into round shapes. There is also volcanic porphyrite and andesite. About thirty kilometers from St. Catherine's Monastery in the direction of Nuweiba, Permian-Triassic sandstone appears and soon dominates the whole landscape. Here the Wadi Arada has carved out a valley, with its *nawamis*, (**Fig. pages 82–83**) five-thousand-year-old stone houses of the Timna civilization, and its frequently visited green oasis of Ain Hudra in the midst of a bizarre sandstone desert. After a steep climb, which affords a wonderful view to the west, there is another region of older granite that suddenly falls steeply away to the depths of the Gulf of Aqaba.

Resuming our north-south journey through the geological history of Sinai, we remain for a moment in the high granite mountains with steep towering peaks of over 2,000 meters and deeply cut wadis between them. Gabal Umm Shomar, at 2,586 meters the second-highest mountain in Sinai, is a precipitous massif and a unique vantage point. From here you have a wonderful view of the Gulf of Suez, the Gulf of Aqaba and the Saudi Arabian mountain coast.

The different structure of the coastal zones that border the central mountains to the west and east cannot be seen yet. West of the massif of Serbal and Umm Shomar lies the wide gravel-sand Qaa Plain, covered with late Pleistocene and recent sediments. Just before al-Tur, the main town in the south, a low mountain ridge (Gabal Araba, Gabal Qabaliat) cordons off the plain from the Gulf of Suez. Further to the south, the Qaa Plain extends right to the sea. At the foot of the coastal mountains, hot sulfuric water

Bands of igneous rocks give the Sinai mountains their particular structure and enliven the landscape.

comes out in a palm grove near al-Tur. These springs are known as Hammam Sayyidna Musa, 'the bath of our Lord Moses.'

Al-Tur is a small seaport with an old tradition. The town is built on a fossil coral reef and its houses are built of coral. The famous zoologist Ernst Haeckel was excited by the well preserved corals in the walls of the houses of the town. For a long time al-Tur was a stopping-place and quarantine station for Mecca pilgrims. Today it is the administrative capital of South Sinai.

The east coast of Sinai is completely different. Here there are scarcely any sandy beaches, as most of the granite mountains plunge steeply and directly into the depths of the Aqaba trench. Only at the few wadi mouths have gravel deltas formed, such as those on which the oases of Nuweiba and Dahab are situated. (The name Dahab means gold, and in fact the beach glitters with innumerable tiny mica flakes.) The location of Dahab and Nuweiba at wadi mouths has its danger. In the last few years, many storm floods in the steep and narrow Wadi Watir have washed away streets in Nuweiba, and the gravel-fields in front of the town are strewn with large granite boulders that have been swept down by raging torrents of water.

From Gabal Umm Shomar the staggered line of the serrate Sinai mountain peaks falls gradually down to the south and turns abruptly into alluvial sand plains at the southern point of the peninsula. But this is not yet the end of Sinai. On an isthmus approximately 700 meters wide and 3.5 kilometers long, our route leads between the mouths of the two gulfs to another highlight of Sinai's landscape, Ras Muhammad. The southern end of the Sinai triangle is well known as one of the best diving places in the world. But Ras Muhammad also has its own geological and ecological peculiarities. At first glance, the fissured, chalky ground appears gray and uninteresting. Closer examination, however, reveals the remains of billions of living things — a fossil coral-reef. The often well-preserved fossils reveal marine organisms that lived from 20 million to 75,000 years ago. Here, marine biologists have the rare chance to compare directly a coral reef from the distant past with a living reef. And this projecting spit of land provides geologists with evidence of the earth's power to create the still-active rift system. In the coral shelf are fissures and clefts that were formed only a few years ago by earthquakes. One of these clefts appears to be very deep and contains seawater.

At Ras Muhammad the Gulf of Suez and the Gulf of Aqaba end and the Red Sea begins. As two very different branches of the same rift system, the gulfs are worth close examination. The Gulf of Suez is broad, but (with a maximum depth of ninety meters) relatively shallow. It is a branch of the great African Rift Valley, which extends from Mozambique in the south to Turkey in the north. The sandy soil of the Gulf of Suez is stirred up and reordered by wind and waves, and the shallow water cools rapidly on cold winter nights. This is why – in contrast to the Gulf of Aqaba – coral reefs cannot survive in the Gulf of Suez. Only in the southern part can a few small isolated reefs be found in very well protected places.

The Gulf of Aqaba is completely different. It fills a narrow trench between Sinai and the Arabian peninsula to a depth of over 1,800 meters, and is not only the northernmost coral sea but also one of the richest and most colorful in the world. Here is an illustration of how a combination of geological features and geographical circumstances can create the determining foundations for life.

These buildings in the old harbor of al-Tur will soon be a thing of the past. They are built of coral. The zoologist Enrst Haeckel, who admired them at the beginning of this century, wrote: "Some of these miserable huts hide a bigger collection of beautiful corals in one single wall than one could find in most European museums. We would have liked to buy the whole village, pack it up and send it home." Today, the houses have become dilapidated and many have already been torn down.

A well-preserved piece of fossil coral that could be almost seventy thousand years old.

Of all the routes across Sinai, the Mediterranean route has always been the most important. The ancient Egyptian Way of Horus became the Roman Via Maris and is the Road of the Philistines, mentioned in the Bible. It has maintained its importance as a trade route and military road between Egypt and Palestine until today. The Darb al-Hagg, last used by a caravan of pilgrims to cross Sinai in 1883, was used by up to ten thousand pious Mecca pilgrims in some years for the nine difficult days of travel.

Opposite page:
The satellite photograph shows the Sinai peninsula from the south. Washed by the Red Sea in the south and the Mediterranean in the north, Sinai appears as a giant wedge squeezed between Africa in the west and Asia in the east. It is clear how the Suez Canal runs from the northern end of the Gulf of Suez through the Bitter Lakes to the Mediterranean. On the north coast the spit of land that divides Lake Bardawil from the Mediterranean can be seen. The formation comprising the deep Gulf of Aqaba, which begins in the south at the narrow Straits of Tiran and ends in the north at Eilat and Aqaba, continues through Wadi Araba to the Dead Sea.

Following pages:
The eastern Sinai mountains fall abruptly and almost vertically down to the Gulf of Aqaba at the Dahab's Southern Oasis. A wadi breaks through the mountain ridge and at its mouth stand the few palm groves of a fabulously beautiful coastal oasis. Only a few meters from the shore, a gloriously colorful coral reef is hidden under the surface of the blue water.

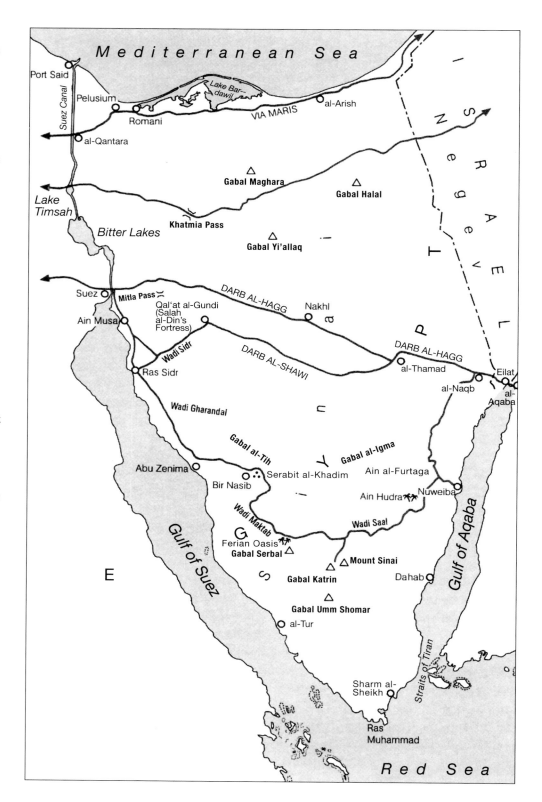

The view of the northern section of the Serbal mountains shows wild, untouched scenery that looks different when the light changes. Steep peaks and sharp ridges emerge through the weathering of younger, hard granites that form the Serbal mountain chain. According to Theodorus of Sicily the name Serbal is derived from Baal, the Mesopotamian god who was also called 'lord of the mountains.' Since the early Christian diocesan town of

Pharan was located behind Mount Serbal in Wadi Feiran, this imposing mountain was often referred to as Mount Horeb.

Following pages:
The hilltop ruins of Saladin's fortress of Qal'at al-Gundi offer a wide view over the Tih Plateau. This arid and highly eroded plain is the biblical "Desert of Confusion."

Opposite:
Liquid basalt broke through the Eocene strata of this limestone mountain (above) behind the Tayiba Oasis and formed a covering black band. The limestone stratum lying underneath was baked red by the great heat of the slowly solidifying stone. Liquid magma filled in the granite clefts and solidified as dikes. Climbing up Gabal Serbal through Wadi Gibba, it can be seen as an exposed black band (below right). The wind-eroded columns in the layered sandstone of Wadi Arada resemble architectural caprices (below left).

This page:
Wind erosion has created a real lunar landscape in the vicinity of the *nawamis* (above). The unassuming desert plant *Anastatica hierochuntica* (left) is the 'real' rose of Jericho. At the top are some seeds, which are ejected by the twigs when it rains. This plant is said to have healing powers – a cold infusion of it allegedly helps in childbirth.

Erosion – by wind in sandstone (above), by temperature in crystalline stone (left), and by water in the sandstone gorge of Wadi Arada (right) – has created the most varied shapes. The narrow gorge of Wadi Arada has been washed out by infrequent but forceful floods that have formed vertical chimneys and openings in the soft sandstone.

On the road, Bedouin offer short camel rides to visit this natural wonder, but to penetrate further into the gorge climbing is necessary.

Rain and meltwater rush down from the high mountains and collect in washed-out stone basins in winter, making wonderful swimming-pools (above) in front of the wonderful mountain backdrop for several months on into the summer. The water serves above all to water the beautiful orchards around Mount Sinai and Gabal Katrin. Sometimes the accumulations of water result from devasta-ting thunderstorms. For days, or for hours, huge but very shallow ponds form, conjuring an unusual landscape. The water seeps away and evaporates quickly, and only fissures in the soil (see next double page) give evidence that lifegiving water once stood there.

Where water has recently evaporated, deposits and fissures create patterns in the sand (above and left). The structures in the sandstone of the Rainbow Canyon can be described as natural works of art (right). Apart from faults and folds, the deposits left by turbulent torrents of water, which frequently changed direction, have created hidden works of art that were later exposed by wind and water erosion.

Following pages:
The constantly blowing wind in the plains of northern Sinai has piled the Sahara sand into huge shifting dunes that migrate unwaveringly, sometimes even burying roads and oases.

In the constant struggle against the wind, plants have to fight against suffocation by the sand on the one hand and against the exposure of their roots on the other (above left). Some plants move with their dune: the exposed back part dies, while the plant grows new roots in the direction of the wind. Perhaps only once in a decade, plentiful rain and favorable temperatures transform the bare sandy wilderness into a multicolored carpet of flowers-the miracle of the blooming desert. The short-lived plants grow and bloom within a few days or weeks and their seeds ripen before the hot desert wind withers them. The splendid yellow inflorescence of the parasitic *Cistanche phelypaea* (right) can be seen every spring, as it takes sustenance from the roots of *Chenopodiaceae* or tamarisks.

An ancient acacia has managed to survive among the large boulders of a wild mountain wadi below the Serbal mountain chain in the face of years of dryness and infrequent turbulent inundations. The acacias provide food and firewood for the human inhabitants of Sinai, who also eat its resin in times of need. Dromedaries and goats eat the fresh acacia branches despite their long, tough thorns.

Above:
The storks'-bill *(Erodium hirtum)*, a member of the geranium family, conjures up such beautiful flowers even in an inhospitable gravel desert.
Below:
The spiny globe thistle *(Echinops spinossisimus)*. This name is the best description for this inconspicuous plant, which becomes a beauty when its blue and white blooms open between the thorns.

Far left:
The caper bush demonstrates the great difficulty of the struggle for survival. A little water in the rock clefts must suffice. The blossoms of the wild caper (middle left) are among the most beautiful blooms in this bleak wilderness.

Above left:
The desert pumpkin, also called *Colocynth*, is used by Bedouin as a very strong laxative. Ripe pumpkins are dry and light, and when they tear off from their mother plant, the wind blows them across the desert like balls, spreading them far and wide. Finally the brittle ball breaks open and its seeds pour out to germinate.

Below left:
Leaf rosette of a Sinaitic mullein. Four of the six *Verbascum* species that exist in Egypt grow only in Sinai.

Above:
Poisonous locusts *(Poekilocerus bufonius)* sitting in henbane *(Hyoscyamus boveanus)*.
The shocking warning color of this locust couple indicates poison, as do the lush green and the conspicuous blooms of the henbane (right).
The poisonous locust eats the henbane and other poisonous plants and stores the poison for protection against predators.

Above left:
This dabb-lizard species *(Uro-mastix ornatus)* is very rare in Sinai, and this individual that has recently shed its skin is an especially beautifully colored specimen. Dabb-lizards are plant-eaters and burrow in the ground. They belong to the agama family.

Left:
The sand snake *(Psammophis schokari)* is a harmless, elegant, slim species of snake that can be commonly seen in Sinai – even among the limestone pillars of the shelters at Ras Muhammad.

Above:
The small and fast moving Sinai agama *(Agama sinaita)* can normally barely be seen among the rocks of wadis, as they adjust their coloring to their environment. In the mating season, however, the male sports a bright turquoise head and sits on the highest boulder to guard its territory and defend it against rivals.

Above: The red fox *(Vulpes vulpes)* in North Africa and Sinai is smaller and lighter and has relatively bigger ears than its European relative. Apart from red foxes and desert foxes, there are also timid and very pale-colored sand foxes *(Vulpes rueppelli).* Other dog-like pedators in Sinai are the striped hyena and common jackal, but both have become very rare through hunting.

Left: Dromedary-breeding is an old privilege of the Bedouin. Humans would not have been able to settle permantently in desert areas without camels. Dromedaries have adapted especially well to the desert. Researchers have found that at least twelve organs of the dromedary show modifications for desert conditions for the purpose of saving water, circulation cooling, food storage, and locomotion on desert ground.

Especially in the vicinity of Sharm al-Sheikh, numerous ospreys *(Pandion haliaetus)* can be observed over the reef-shelf hunting for fish.
Right:
The western reef heron *(Egretta gularis)* is difficult to distinguish from the little egret *(E. garzetta)*, as both species can be black as well as white. The specimen shown here could not decide between white and black.

Following pages: Tens of thousands of storks covered the Mangrove Island of Ras Muhammad in August 1988. Storks are not the only birds that use Sinai as an important resting place on their way south. Regularly in spring and late summer, migrating raptors, herons, seagulls, and numerous species of small birds can be observed. The migration of quails is mentioned in the Bible.

Left:
The promontory of Ras Muhammad offers a marvelous view of the Sinai mountains.
The aerial photograph (top) shows Ras Muhammad with the Mangrove Channel and the well-known Shark Point. The promontory is the southern point of the Sinai peninsula and has recently been designated a national park.

The Gordon Reef (middle) is one of the most beautiful diving sites in the Straits of Tiran. The mangroves that grow on the reef shelf at Wadi Kid (bottom) are the northernmost in the world.

Above:
A hole in the reef shelf is one entrance to the coral world of Ras Muhammad.
Right:
Soft corals *(Dendronephthya spec.)* and a Gorgonian sea fan *(Acabaria spec.)* do not belong to the reef-forming stone corals but contribute substantially to the beauty of the 'magic gardens' of the Red Sea.

Following pages:
Butterfly fish and emperor fish are among the most gloriously colorful coral fishes. The masked butterfly fish (*Chaetodon semilarvatus;* above left) normally appear in pairs. In some classification books, the queen angelfish (*Pomacanthus maculosus;* below left) is confused with the Arabian angelfish (*Pomacanthus asfur),* which is rare in the northern Red Sea. The emperor fish (*Pomacanthus imperator;* above right) lives throughout the Indo-Pacific area.
Below right:
No book on coral fish fails to mention the well-known symbiosis between sea anemones and anemone fish of the genus *Amphiprion.* Less well known is the fact that the young three-spotted coral fish *(Dascyllus trimaculatus)* shown here can also seek protection among the stinging tentacles of sea anemones without being eaten.

Above:
The giant butterfly fish *(Chae-todon lineolatus)* with a length of thirty centimeters is the largest of its genus. This species is scattered throughout the Indo-Pacific but quite rare in the Red Sea.
Right:
Fire corals *(Millepora dicho-toma)*, soft corals *(Dendronepht-hya spec.)*, and sponges of the genera *Cliona* (red) and *Gray-ella* (whitish) build a filigree archway on a reef pillar.
Following pages:
Beware! The beautiful sponge of the genus *Latrunculia* (above left) is poisonous. The mag-nificent giant squirrelfish *(Adioryx spinifer;* below left) can be found under over-hanging rocks and in caves. The orange-spotted jack *(Carangoides bajad;* above right) is one of the fast-swim-ming open-sea predators that also frequent the reef. The species shown here is usually silver-colored with orange-

yellow spots, but occasionally it can turn completely yellow. The coral grouper *(Chepha-lopholis miniata;* below right) is one of the most magnificent fish in the reef. Groupers are represented by many species in coral seas. Large specimens can grow to as much as two meters in length.

Above:
There are several species of marine turtles in the Red Sea. The specimen shown here is probably a loggerhead sea turtle *(Chelone mydas)*, which, unlike other species, also eats seaweed. All species of marine turtles are endangered because of hunting and disturbance of their nesting sites.
Left:
The manta ray is the biggest ray. A plankton-eater, it can grow to up to seven meters wide. A high-sea fish, it comes only rarely to the reef.

A remora has attached itself firmly to the manta ray's back. As long as divers and snorkelers remain calm, manta rays are not too shy. It is a unique underwater experience to be circled around at very closely by these elegant giants.

Above:
The napoleon fish *(Cheilinus undulatus)* can grow to up to two meters long and 190 kilograms in weight. Nevertheless, it is a harmless reef inhabitant belonging to the wrasse family, a very varied group. Apart from fish it eats sea urchins, mollusks, crabs, and other invertebrates. Adult napoleon fish males have a large hump on the forehead.

Right:
A stonefish *(Synanceia verrucosa).* About fifty centimeters away from this animal lay a second stonefish which we had photographed several times before we discovered this specimen. This photograph without flash shows the perfect camouflage and with it the great danger that attends these extremely poisonous fishes. The poisonous stingers on fins and opercula can cause very painful injuries, and deaths have been recorded. This example shows that for their own safety people should never touch anything in the reef.

Above:
The fire lionfish *(Pterois radiata)* belongs, together with the closely-related lionfish *(Pterois volitans)*, among the strangest fish in the reef. Only seldom can its highly-developed hunting behavior be observed, when several animals cooperate. Then together they encircle a swarm of small fish in a bay. As with the stonefish, the spines of fire lionfish are connected to dangerous venomous glands.

Right:
All stone and soft corals are filterers that sieve plankton from the water for nourishment. The great sea fan *(Subergorgia hicksoni)* in the lower right corner of the picture is well adapted for this.

Above and above right:
At a reef wall a leopard
grouper *(Plectropomus pessuli-
ferum)* lies in wait with bared
teeth. In spite of its unfriendly
appearance, this grouper is
harmless to humans. A small
cleaner wrasse *(Labroides
dimidiatus)* rids the big predator of parasites. Against
a lighter background, the
grouper's coloring becomes
lighter too.

Below right:
The poisonous bearded
scorpionfish *(Scorpaenopsis
barbatus)* belongs to the same
family as stonefish and fire-
fish. Unlike stonefish, scorpionfish have a more vivid
coloring and move more
often. Nevertheless, they are
very well camouflaged and
may easily be overlooked.

Following pages:
Like a cloud, a shoal of scalefin anthiases *(Anthias squami-
pinnis)* at a depth of twenty-
five meters surrounds a coral
covered with soft corals *(Dendronephthya spec.).* Scalefin
anthiases undergo a strange
kind of sex change. If too
many of the large, beautiful
males are eaten, the strongest
females transform themselves
into males within a few hours.

Ecology

Flora and Fauna on the Land Bridge Between Africa and Asia

Soil and climate determine the occurrence and spread of plants and animals. This fundamental ecological tenet assigns to geology and geography an important role in the survival of plants and animals. The ecology of Sinai, as well as the marine biology of the Red Sea, demonstrate this very clearly. On land, the paucity of species in the spatially restricted Sinai area creates clear-cut relationships. In the Red Sea, the geological formation of the seabed and the geographical location are the decisive factors.

Observation of the flora and fauna in Sinai makes it clear that the peninsula is a genuine land bridge between Africa and Eurasia. Here plant species from four major neighboring regions mix.

Most of the plants belong to the Sahara-Arabian region. The most important and best-known species are the camelthorn *(Zilla spinosa)*, the various kinds of goosefoot *(Hammada spec, Anabasis spec)* and bean capers *(Zygophyllum spec.)*, and tamarisks *(Tamarix spec.)*. The biblical story of manna, the bread from heaven, is associated with the tamarisk. This legend, handed down by Sinai monks, comes close to being a miracle, since the manna harvest is very scant and only very seldom possible. Manna is the honey-like excretion of lice, which pierce the capillary tubes of tamarisk branches. At first the drops are crystal-clear, then they turn milky and finally brownish.

From the Sudanese region come the acacia, the caper bush, the ben-oil tree *(Moringa peregrina)*, *Leptadenia pyrotechnica*, and the poisonous Sodom-apple *(Calotropis procera)*, which can all be found mainly in the warm lowlands of the gulfs. In the coastal waters of the Gulf of Aqaba and at Ras Muhammad grows the mangrove *(Avicennia marina)*, its northernmost location in the world. Persian and North African grassland species like primula *(Primula boveana)* and pistachio *(Pistacea atlantica)* grow in the cooler and more humid climate of higher mountains and plateaus. Surprisingly, only a few species of Mediterranean flora can be found in Sinai, in spite of that region's proximity. In former times Mediterranean plants were widespread in Sinai, but now they persist only in specific places. This indicates a changing climate that long ago made Sinai drier and drier, a phenomenon evident in the neighboring Sahara as well. Limited Mediterranean species are the Phoenician juniper *(Juniperus phoenicea)*, which can be found at the rare places with plenty of water in North Sinai, the sand cherry *(Ephedra campylopoda)* and the olive tree *(Olea europaea)*. Marjoram *(Origanum isthmicum)* has a very small range of distribution of only five square kilometers on Gabal Halal.

Zoogeographically, Sinai is full of overlaps and intersections that have created an interesting mixture of fauna. Since animals, unlike plants, can move – and in some cases quickly cover long distances – the boundaries cannot be as sharply drawn as for flora (**Fig. page 42**).

Beside wolves, ibexes, red foxes, dormice, partridges, and rock doves from the southern Palearctic region, there are also species typical of the

A branch of a tamarisk *(Tamarix nilotica)* with manna.

Left:
Water is always of great importance in the desert. In spring the water stays longer in mountain wadis than in the plains, so that even algae can grow, but soon the heat dries up the rivulet. Under the sand the water continues to flow for a long time yet, and the Bedouin know that they can dig wells successfully here.

tropical African region such as Tristram's grackle *(Onychognathus tristramii)*, the common bulbul *(Pycnonotus leucogenys)*, the sunbird *(Nectarinia osaea)*, and the rodent-like relative of the elephant, the rock hyrax *(Procavia syriaca)*. In former times there were ostriches here. Sometimes their eggs are still found in the desert sand. Leopards, only recently exinct, as well as hyenas and jackals, must have crossed the Sinai land bridge as they spread to Asia. In Sinai the dull-colored partridge *(Perdix perdix)*, which lives mainly in northwestern Europe, meets the brightly-colored chukar *(Alectoris chukar)*, which lives mainly in southeastern Europe, Arabia, and Persia.

A main characteristic of Sinai's flora and fauna is their poverty of species. The total number of species of ferns and flowering plants is recorded as 820–900, including thirty-four endemic species found only in Sinai. In comparison, more than 1,400 species are estimated to exist in the Sahara, and that number of species could be found in a tropical rain forest in an area only a few kilometers square. The situation is similar for animals, though there are no reliable data available.

The small number of species is a direct consequence of climatic factors. Life-threatening water shortages combine with high temperatures by day, extreme variation in temperature between day and night, and the effects of wind to make every habitat an extreme one. In the desert water is the factor that determines the survival of animals and plants. Even in places with occasionally plentiful water, difficult living conditions prevail. Due to high evaporation, the dissolved soil minerals accumulate and the water becomes very salty. Consequently, desert inhabitants – whether plants, animals, or humans – have had to adapt and develop strategies of survival in order to settle permanently. When species that do not have these adaptations are found in such an environment, two explanations are possible. Either there are better living conditions within a restricted area, or the last representatives of a species are eking out a miserable existence as so-called relict species, witnesses of a formerly humid climate. In Sinai, examples of such species are the Mediterranean plants and water insects such as *Gyrinidae* and *Dytiscus* species, water scorpions, and dragonflies, as well as water snails of the family *Lymnaeidae*, which to our surprise we found in the winter rain ponds of mountain wadis.

Individual adaptations to desert life can be inferred by observing the plants and animals. Open spacing between plants is an expression of the struggle for water. Even very small plants may develop superficial root systems of up to one hundred square meters in order to use the scant, barely absorbed water. There is simply no place in between for other plants. Alternatively, larger plants develop deep roots in order to reach the ground water. (**Fig. page 36–37**) Acacias with roots reaching down thirty-five meters have been found. Before an acacia can grow to this size it has to succeed in a hard struggle for survival. First of all, the seed needs enough water for germination. If the young plant grows well in a succession of good years, it is exposed to numerous feeders like gazelles, goats, and camels, which crave the fresh green and hinder growth. Even the long, hard, sharp thorns do not keep them off. If a few rain-poor years follow, the dream of a beautiful big acacia is over.

Sand provides fairly good water storage, so many plants are shaped to favor the collection of sand: they catch the windblown sand and build their own sandhills. Sometimes whole areas are covered with these hillocks with plants growing out like tufts of hair. Such areas can be seen on the drive to al-Tur south of Ras Sidr.

The outward shape of many desert plants results from their effort to minimize evaporation, which, given the high temperatures and strong wind, is a critical problem. Small leaves, round shapes, and stocky statures are examples of this effort. The widespread bright green and very lush-seeming Syrian bean capers of the genus *Zygophyllum*, which belong to the succulents, show this adaptation very clearly. Their leaves have become round and juicy with smooth surfaces.

The Syrian bean capers are real masters of adaptation because they have developed a number of mechanisms to survive successfully in the desert. Another way to minimize evaporation is to absorb water-binding salt into cell liquids. Desert water contains more than enough salt, but in the Syrian bean caper, the salt concentration is three times as high as in the desert water, which is already intolerably salty for 'normal' plants. With the high concentration of salt in their leaves, the Syrian bean capers are able to absorb even tiny amounts of dew moisture through their stomata and so attain a regular water supply. And there is a third strategy of the Syrian bean caper to minimize evaporation. Like every foliage plant it takes up carbon dioxide from the air through its stomata for photosynthesis. In the heat of the day, open stomata would lead to high evaporation, so the Syrian bean caper takes up carbon dioxide at night, stores it chemically, and keeps its stomata closed during the day.

Meanwhile, sodium chloride can cause problems even for salt-tolerant plants, as too much of it damages the tissue. To prevent this, a number of species have developed glands in the leaves and stems that excrete salt, creating little crystals on the surface. These crystals effectively reflect the sunlight and thus serve as further protection from evaporation. The salt-wort species of the genus *Salsola*, normally rather inconspicuous, stands out because of the tiny glittering white crystals on its small blue-green leaves. The well-known tamarisks with their needle-like branches and twigs are covered with a whitish coating that reveals itself as sodium chloride when tasted.

A few examples of from the animal kingdom may complete this short discussion of strategies for survival in the desert. Dabb-lizards (**Fig. page 40**), large, monitor-like reptiles, are dark grayish-black in the morning. As the heat intensifies through the day, they change their color to gray-green or paler and finally to pale gray or even white. In the coolness of the morning, they gather warmth through their dark color. Later, the pale tinge prevents overheating by reflecting light. These impressive animals have further peculiarities that make their lives in the desert easier. They have salt glands in their nostrils that excrete almost-dry salt. By doing so, they retain water, which they would otherwise have to use to excrete salt through their kidneys. The dabb-lizards protect themselves against predators by squeezing tightly into crevices. In order to do this, they have air sacs behind their lungs which they pump up. Interestingly, these air sacs actually have another function: they are used to allow the air to circulate twice through the lungs. The oxygen content is therefore better utilized, and the breathing rate can be slowed, reducing water evaporation.

The surprisingly numerous black beetles use color to similar effect. Although black may seem quite unsuitable for a hot sunny desert, in the morning after a starlit desert night when the temperature can fall quite low, the

Trace of a dab-lizard in the sand.

beetles' black color helps to absorb warmth, allowing them to get moving more quickly. Later when the day becomes too hot they bury themselves in sand. This is the only relief for a number of desert animals. Skinks, lizard-like reptiles, have adapted their body shape so that with their shiny, smooth, scaly skin they are able to 'swim' in the sand. The eyelids of skinks, as well as those of desert lizards, are transparent and protect their eyes like sand-goggles. The horned viper and its relatives have another solution to the problem of loose sand. By moving in sideways curves, these poisonous desert vipers worm their way through the sand and avoid unintentional sinking, crossing even the softest places.

Many desert animals of different families camouflage themselves by adjusting their color to their surroundings. Hoopoe larks, coursers, or golden spiny mice are often first noticed when they run away. The normally conspicuous black-and-white male of the white-crowned black wheatear, for example, looks like a stone with a shadow in the high midday sun. It sits motionless on the ground and is first recognized as a bird when it flies up. The sand-gray female of the wheatear is even better camouflaged, and when incubating eggs she can be hardly distinguished from her environment. Frequently lizards scurry unexpectedly away before our feet, or grasshoppers fly up, so perfectly are both animals camouflaged against the ground by color and pattern. This is necessary as the open areas with scant vegetation are good hunting grounds for predators. The predator easily becomes the prey when a stronger predator approaches.

On the other hand, sometimes there are conspicuous, brightly colored species in the desert, like the black and brilliant orange grasshopper *(Poekilocerus bufonius)*. (**Fig. page** 39) This grasshopper is extremely poisonous because it eats poisonous plants like French cotton or henbane. It not only tolerates but actually concentrates the poison. The conspicuous color warns possible predators and scares them off.

From an ecological point of view, one gets to know both the large biospheres of Sinai when wandering through the Tih desert in the north and the mountain zone in the south. The geological variety of Sinai creates such varied local habitats that these biospheres must be further subdivided in order to understand their colonization by flora and fauna.

Northern Sinai

A first distinct area is the Mediterranean coast, with the adjoining dune belt. Due to the proximity of the sea, fairly regular rain and dew provide enough water, and sand stores water well. On the north side of the dunes especially, the wild plants have been so displaced by the intensification of agriculture that at first they are hardly noticeable. Where agriculture becomes less important, species such as different grasses *(Ammophila arenaria, Panicum turgidum, Cynodon dactylon)*, knotweed *(Polygonum equisetiforme)*, and birds'-foot trefoil (Lotus creticus) dominate the plant community.

The Tih Plateau, with its seemingly endless fields of gravel and scree, takes up the largest part of northern Sinai. Wide areas appear to have no flora or fauna. Only by looking more closely can isolated traces of life be found. The determining factor is water. Wherever even tiny amounts of water collect, vegetation, albeit stunted, appears. Sparse vegetation follows the depression of Wadi al-Arish and its countless branches. There – beside ubiquitous plants like camelthorn, glasswort *(Chenopodiaceae)*, the *Hammada* and *Anabasis* species, and the Syrian bean caper of the genus *Zygophyllum* – also grow the niter bush *(Nitraria retusa)*, mugwort *(Artemisia inculta)*, and saltwort *(Salsola tetranda, S. inermis)*. Thorny acacias grow in places with higher groundwater. (**Fig. pages 36–37**)

One plant only a few centimeters high can easily be overlooked in the gravel because it appears to be dead or might be mistaken for a stone due to its gray and tiny bent branches. It is the famous rose of Jericho *(Anastatica hierochuntica)*, (**Fig. page 25**) which when it rains unfolds its bent branches and twigs within minutes, thereby releasing its ripe seeds for germination.

The isolated mountain ranges rising out of the Tih Plateau are especially interesting for botanists, as this is where some of the relic plants are found. More frequent rainfall and dew provide better and more regular water.

Dunes and sandy areas far from the coast form a distinct region in the Tih desert, as here also a better water supply is guaranteed through the storage ability of the sand. On shifting dunes, plants are confronted with another serious problem: the wind blows the soil away from the roots or threatens to bury the plant. A countermeasure of some grass species especially is an extensive root system for holding the sand in place, as well as vegetative propagation by long runners.

As a highlight of desert flora, a few plants should be mentioned that create the wonder of a flowering desert after the infrequent heavy rainfalls. A real flowering (**Fig. pages 34–35**) carpet can be created by *Diplotaxis acris*, with its violet blossoms, and the yellow blossoms of the stinkweed *(Diplotaxis harra)*. Among them can be seen the marguerite-like chamomiles of the genus *Anthemis*, the yellow adonis *(Adonis dentatus)*, red- or violet-blooming storksbill species of the genera *Geranium* and *Erodium*, and the conspicuous yellow inflorescences of the parasitic plant *Cistanche phelypaea*, (**Fig. page 35**) and the even brighter yellow blooms of other compositae. All of these are transcended by the bright red of the poppy *(Papaver rhoeas)*.

Southern Sinai

A brief overview of this region is more difficult, as southern Sinai encompasses numerous diverse habitats through its geological variety and the dramatic differences in altitude ranging from sea level up to 2,600 meters. Preferred locations for plants are the sandy gravel lowland plains and the mountain wadis, which are often surprisingly well watered. In the granite mountains at least sparse vegetation grows in clefts and gaps almost all the way up to the peaks. The sandstone mountains, in contrast, are normally barren, as here the water drains off and seeps away quickly.

Numerous strong-smelling herbs and medicinal plants are characteristic of wadis in the mountain zone, giving one the feeling of wandering through a herbalist's shop. Species of mugwort *(Artemisia inculta, A. monosperma)* are widespread, as are oregano, mint, rosemary, anise, sage, lavender, and milfoil. Also characteristic is the endemic species of Sinaitic mullein *(Verbascum sinaiticum)* with its nearly human-high, branched stalks bearing many yellow blossoms growing out of a ground level rosette of leaves. Other plants spread throughout southern Sinai are the rare wick weed *(Phlomis aureea)* belonging to the *Labiatae*, another *Labiata* called *Micromeria serbaliana*, the Sinaitic St. John's wort *(Hypericum sinaicum)* and the Cotoneaster *(Cotoneaster*

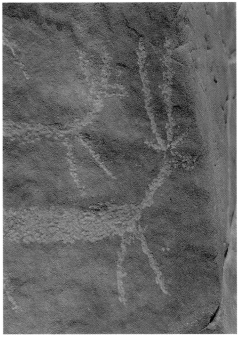

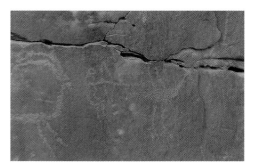

Rock pictures can give clues about extinct animal species that once existed in Sinai. At one time there could have been giraffes. It is certain anyway that in the last century white oryxes and ostriches were hunted in Sinai. Ostrich eggs were also used as Christian symbols in St. Catherine's Monastery (see the picture on page 89).

orbicularis). The typical tree in the wadis is the very thorny acacia *(Acacia raddiana)*.

Even the shortest discussion of Sinai's plant world cannot be concluded without mentioning the 'burning thornbush' in St. Catherine's Monastery. Photographs from before the Israeli occupation show that a Syrian senna tree *(Colutea istria)* grew at this historic spot, whereas what grows there today is a species of blackberry *(Rubus sanctus)*, probably descended from a cultivated form.

Observing animals is more difficult in the desert than elsewhere and requires more patience and persistence. Almost every animal is well camouflaged, very shy, and avoids the heat of the day. Above all, the big mammals are hunted in large numbers, especially since the Bedouin too have acquired rifles and cross-country vehicles. Some species are on the verge of extinction or have already been exterminated, especially since hunters from among the European and American experts resident in Egypt help to make the situation worse. Species that are already extinct are the leopard and the ostrich. Wolves, striped hyenas, and dorcas gazelles are almost extinct. Whether the announced regulations can still save the Nubian ibex is doubtful. Even the hyrax can rarely be seen since the Bedouin have recently begun hunting and eating it. According to a report by E. H. Palmer in 1872, in the past the Bedouin considered the hyrax to be an ancestor of human beings because its feet are shaped like human hands, and they avoided eating its flesh, for according to legend whoever did so would never be able to look their parents in the eye again. Since that time this taboo seems to have been forgotten.

The red fox *(Vulpes vulpes)* is a widespread mammal and often confused with the desert fox *(Fennecus zerda)*. The red fox in desert areas is smaller and lighter and clearly has bigger ears than its European cousin, but the desert fox, or fennec, is even smaller and has proportionally even bigger ears.

As in European culture, the fox plays an important role in Sinai's folklore. A nice example of such folktales was recorded by C. B. Klunzinger in 1878: A fox wanted the chicks a man was taking to market in a basket. The fox ran on ahead, lay down on the way and pretended to be dead. When the man passed, he hardly noticed the fox. The fox repeated his trick twice more. Finally, the man thought to himself that three fox skins were worth selling in the market. He put his basket down and went back to collect the two previous dead foxes, but he could not find them. When he came back to his basket, not only had the fox disappeared but also the chicks with him.

Most of the mammals of Sinai belong to the rodent family, but they are rarely seen due to their hidden and mostly nocturnal lifestyle. Lesser jerboas and gerbils belong to the most common species. In the ruins of the temple of Serabit al-Khadim golden spiny mice of the genus Acomys can be observed, the church mice of the ancient Egyptians, so to speak.

Sinai's bird community is very interesting. Inland the brown-necked raven *(Corvus ruficollis)* and the white-crowned black wheater *(Oenanthe leucopyga)* belong to the most important species. The courser *(Cursorius cursor)*, the hoopoe lark *(Alaemon alaudipes)*, and the trumpeter finch *(Bucanetes githagineus)* show special adjustment to the desert through their coloring. The Egyptian vulture *(Neophron percnopterus)*, the tawny eagle *(Aquila rapax)*, and the griffon vulture *(Gypus fulvus)* are seen rarely. More common are various species of falcons, among them the barbary falcon *(Falco pelegrinoides)*, similar to the peregrine falcon.

On the coasts both the white-eyed gull *(Larus leucophthalmus)* and the sooty gull *(Larus hemprichii)* are frequent and can easily be confused. Among several species of heron there is the western reef heron *(Egretta gularis)*, which occurs in black as well as white. (**Fig. page 43**) A nearly tame cattle egret *(Bubulcus ibis)* lived on Ras Muhammad for years. As long as camping was allowed there, we appreciated it very much when the egret hopped around on our breakfast table and caught the extremely annoying flies. Similar to the heron is the smaller, brown-patterned bittern *(Botaurus stellaris)*. The streamlined brown booby *(Sula leucogaster)* is a real tropical seabird species, which very seldom appears in the northern Red Sea. On one occasion we also observed a red-billed tropicbird *(Phaethon aethereus)* on the coast of Ras Umm Sid at Sharm al-Sheikh. This white sea bird with its long tail feathers and its bright red beak is a real child of the tropics. The beautiful osprey *(Pandion haliaetus)* can be observed much more often fishing over the reef shelf. (**Fig. page 43**) It builds its nests in the masts of ships run aground in the Straits of Tiran.

The annual bird migration in spring and fall is a fascinating phenomenon. Eastern and southern Sinai belong to the most important bird migration routes. It is a very special experience to see flocks of storks circling in the thermals. For a few days in August in some years large parts of Ras Muhammad are almost covered with storks. (**Fig. pages 44−45**) Between them sit single pelicans, different species of herons, terns (among them the impressive royal tern), and sometimes even small groups of black storks. Normally the migration of an interesting variety of raptor species follows a few days later. Many small birds fly over Sinai as well – the migration of quails is even mentioned in the Bible. Wagtails can frequently be observed, and it is surprising to suddenly come across the bluethroat (*Cyanosylvia svecica*) in dreary desert wadis.

Desert wanderers are also interested in reptiles. By far the most common reptiles in Sinai are lizards of the Acanthodactylus genus of fringe-toed lizards and the desert-racer *(Mesalina)*. The latter does live up to its name. To the smaller lizards belong several gecko species, among them the well-known Hasselquist's fan-footed gecko *(Ptychodactylus hasselquisti)* and the agama. (**Fig. page 41**) In the mating season the male agamas have conspicuous bright turquoise blue heads. The desert monitor and various species of dabb-lizards are large but very shy reptiles.

Approximately twenty different species of snakes have been recorded in Sinai, among them six poisonous species. Only one snake might be sighted regularly, the harmless and elegant sand snake *(Psammophis schokari)*. When it comes to poisonous snakes, the most common are the horned viper *(Cerastes cerastes)* and the closely related lesser cerastes viper *(Cerastes vipera)*. Although we have lived in Egypt for many years and hiked through the desert many times, we have never seen the beautiful but also very poisoness diurnal carpet viper *(Echis pyramidum)* or the large, black Innes' cobra *(Walterinesia aegyptica)*. Wariness of snakes and scorpions is in order during any stay in the desert, but there is no need for excessive fear.

Insects and spiders-both with large numbers of species and individuals-are ecologically important animals in Sinai. Typical forms are the *Tenebrionidae*, the large, voracious, nocturnal Solifugae, and scorpions. The number of very beautifully colored dragonflies is surprisingly high.

This rather incomplete overview of Sinai's flora and fauna and its ecological web can only hope to stimulate the reader's own discoveries.

The ghost crab *(Ocypode saratan)* lives on sandy beaches, where it digs burrows. It can run sideways very quickly. In the picture we can see its extended complex eyes, which can fold down to the side. The sight elements are so arranged around the eye stalk that the ghost crab can see all round.

Marine biology

In the Coral Gardens of the Red Sea

Coming from al-Tur we had just crossed the hot southern Qaa Plain. At a sharp left curve we left the road to continue our journey on a sandy track. After about fifteen kilometers a military post let us pass as we showed the necessary permission from the police station in al-Tur. We had arrived at Ras Muhammad, the southern tip of Sinai. Now the track split into several branches and we followed one of these across a rough, fissured, and bleak limestone plain until our way suddenly ended at a little bay. Before us lay the deep blue water of the Red Sea. Equipped with diving mask and snorkel, we swam over the reef shelf. The first coral and fish appeared before us and the underwater landscape became more and more impressive. Suddenly our breath was taken away: through clouds of innumerable multi-colored fish we could look between stunning corals straight down to the seemingly endless blue depths of the sea. For one brief moment we thought we were falling, but then our attention was caught once again by the unbelievable variety of colors and forms in the reef of Ras Muhammad.

It is hard to imagine more disparate biospheres than the gray and desolate limestone desert of Ras Muhammad and the coral reef of the Red Sea almost exploding with life and color. Complete strangers, leaving the water after their first dive, have come to us and as though under duress simply burst out with their experiences and impressions. Although we have seen many other very beautiful coral reefs, we agree with the opinion of numerous experienced divers that Ras Muhammad is one of the best diving sites in the world. Yet according to normal standards, there should not be any coral reef here at all.

Like every living thing, coral makes certain demands on its environment, and if one single condition is not met, it cannot survive. These conditions include warm, clear, sun-flooded, and nutrient-poor sea water, with a temperature of not less than 18–20° centigrade even in the cold season, and a hard floor where the coral can attach itself firmly. The nutrient-poor factor seems strange at first, but is understandable in light of the fact that highly nutritious waters are generally cloudy. For corals it is most important that the sunlight penetrates deep into the water. The conditions for coral are fulfilled in a belt of varying width around the equator, especially on the eastern coasts of the continents. Due to the earth's rotation the warm water on the sea's surface normally flows westward and therefore strikes the eastern coasts.

So it is rather astonishing that the Red Sea meets these environmental conditions; it is after all a small sea located quite far north. The artful interplay of geological and geographical factors is responsible. The deep rift system has split the old basement complex in the Red Sea, as well as in the Gulf of Aqaba, the miniature version of the Red Sea, thereby creating the hard bottom surface for corals. Due to its location in the Afro-Asian desert belt there is little fertile land around or freshwater inflow, so no nutrients are washed into the sea to cloud the water. The hot desert climate heats up the water sufficiently in the summer. On cold, clear, winter nights, the thermal radiation into space is so high that the water should in theory cool down too much. But even here, the combination of geological circumstances and climatic factors is helpful: the Red Sea and the Gulf of Aqaba lie on a north-south axis. Their southern ends are both nearly closed by straits, the Bab al-Mandab and the Straits of Tiran. Moreover, there is a high rise in the sea floor at both straits. The north winds that predominate in the region push the surface water, which becomes very warm in the summer, to the south all year round. In the straits it meets the high sea floor and to a large extent is forced downward. Thus even at a depth of one thousand meters the water can be an unusually high 20° centigrade. In the depths, the water is gradually pushed to the north, where it finally comes to the surface. In this manner the water circulates, supplying sufficiently warm water year-round-in winter the cold surface water is carried to the south and down toward the bottom and is replaced by warm deep water in the north. No coral sea can develop in the shallow Gulf of Suez, since such water circulation is impossible and since disturbed sand constantly covers the coral.

The coral builders of the reefs are unusual creatures in several respects. Being *Coelenterata*, they belong to the most primitive of multicelled animals, but with their tentacles and stinging cells they control the most complex cells to be found in the animal kingdom. Due to their stationary way of life and their simple structure, corals were for a long time thought to be plants. The single, usually microscopically small polyp consists of a sacklike body enclosed by a wall consisting of an exterior and an interior cell layer with a relatively thick gelatinous supporting lamella in between. Serving as both mouth and excretory organ, the only orifice of the body lies at the upper end, inside a ring of six or eight movable tentacles. The entire exterior wall and the tentacles are covered by stinging cells for catching tiny plankton organisms.

An individual polyp reproduces asexually through budding. Since the young polyp remains attached to the parent polyp through a connective tissue throughout its life, over the years a large colony of polyps is formed, which together create a coral skeleton. To do this, however, the ability to produce limestone is also necessary. The ability to synthesize limestone really is an outstanding achievement as it enables the polyps not only to build calcareous cups to which they can retract in time of danger but also creates the foundation for the genesis of one of the most multi-faceted and species-rich living communities in the world. Coral reefs are the largest natural structures that exist. The Great Barrier Reef alone, along the eastern coast of Australia, is over two thousand kilometers long; and in the course of the earth's history fossil coral reefs have been folded upward to become mountains.

The limestone excretion of polyp colonies is a biologically very interesting process that was first investigated in the late 1950s and early 1960s by the German-American scientist Goreau. What distinguished his research was his observation that coral polyps live in symbiosis with single-celled algae, the *Zooxanthellae*. These algae are responsible for the colorfulness of many corals. Their real importance, however, lies in their use of the carbonic acid formed during limestone production for photosynthesis. If the carbonic acid were not immediately removed, it would dissolve the newly formed limestone. This is why limestone formation takes place only in the daytime, when the algae produce their nutrients through photosynthesis with the help of sunlight. And it is also the reason that coral reefs can only grow in clear, sunlit water.

The growth rate of a coral is difficult to express in numbers. Young corals grow faster than old ones, branched types grow faster than compact types. The temperature also plays a role: optimal growth takes place at a temperature of about 25–27° centigrade. Generally, the growth rate amounts to only a few centimeters per year, so every piece of coral broken is a loss. Reef damage occurs when too many divers and snorkelers touch corals, trample them, or break them off.

The effects of the symbiosis between polyps and algae extend much further. As a waste product of photosynthesis the algae produce large amounts of oxygen, which the whole reef community needs to breathe. Since the oxygen is emitted in a fine form, the sea water is supersaturated to well above 100 percent. This is one of the reasons why coral fish and other reef organisms cannot be kept in an aquarium without difficulty, since they are accustomed to an unusually high oxygen concentration.

Now it is may be understood why the lack of nutrients in the sea water is not a problem for the maintainence of the gigantic reef community. The symbiotic algae produce many more nutrients by photosynthesis than they can use and, with the surplus, feed the polyps. The polyps, for their part, filter particular compounds out of the sea water that the algae need to live. So has arisen a true symbiosis, a genuine partnership based on mutual dependence and assistance.

Not all corals are able to create limestone, mainly just the *Hexacorallia (six-tentacled species)*. The *Octocorallia*, with eight tentacles, are among the most beautifully colored and variously formed soft corals, but not among the reef-creating species. Like other stationary species of sponges, lime-corals, or mussels, they compete for space and, by spreading too much, they may even inhibit the growth of stone corals. Under good growing conditions, stone corals build a real labyrinth of holes, tunnels, channels and grottos of every size, which offer other organisms of very different species countless hiding places and homes. This is one of the most important requirements for a particularly species-rich community, since a highly diverse range of organisms find their ecological niches.

In addition to asexual reproduction through budding from the body wall, coral polyps also reproduce sexually. Depending on the species, polyps can exist as separate sexes or hermaphrodites. In each case, they produce sex cells in their interior cell layer that are deposited in the stomach hole. Sperm are expelled in masses by all polyps at certain times and are filtered from the sea water by polyps of the same species and transported to the stomach. The sperm fertilize the polyps' egg cells and within a few days tiny, free-swimming planula have developed. Remarkably, the egg cells of the mother polyp transfer to the larvae some of the symbiotic algae that are essential later for building new corals. The larvae are expelled simultaneously by all polyps of a coral or a species, and in such amounts that milky clouds can form over whole reef walls. The larvae augment the plankton and are in large part eaten by plankton-eaters such as the manta ray, which

Although the fossil coral (below) with the small fossilized sea urchin has been dead for perhaps one hundred thousand years, its limestone stucture can be seen almost as well as that of the living coral (above). Almost the entire coast of the southern point of Sinai consists of fossil coral limestone.

can grow to seven meters broad. Only the few larvae that survive and find a good surface to attach to can transform themselves into polyps. This tiny, lonely polyp begins with limestone excretion and asexual budding and builds a new coral in the course of time.

Sexual reproduction through larvae helps corals to spread, which explains how these animals came from the Indian Ocean to the rift system of the Red Sea, which emerged later.

There are different reef types, which vary in their construction. In the Red Sea, as well as in the Gulf of Aqaba, there are mainly fringing reefs, extending from the coasts. This is because the narrow but deep rift provides the shoreline with a hard bottom and sunlit water. The corals grew from here into the open sea and developed the present structure of the fringing reef. Close to the beach, the reef top consisting of dead coral limestone is covered by only a few centimeters of water and at ebb tide lies exposed. Further out to sea the first stunted corals can be seen ardously eking out an existence. Behind these, the corals become more numerous and better developed as the reef crown is approached. Here, at the front edge of the reef, with abundant light and waves, the corals have the best growing conditions. In many places, the reef crown extends forward into the open sea over the steep reef wall. The reef walls are covered, especially in the upper parts, with flourishing corals, and even downward the coral growth in the Red Sea diminishes very slowly, a consequence of the clear water. It has been ascertained that the photosynthesis of the symbiotic *Zooxanthellae* still functions at a depth of fifty meters and in extreme cases even at a depth of ninety meters.

When the reef wall does not immediately fall steeply to great depths but forms gentle slopes or terraced steps, wonderful coral towers can grow to several meters high, reaching sometimes almost to the water surface. On broad reef tops, sunken areas on the coastal side of the reef crown create lagoons where corals grow as well. Since the lagoon is not very deep and usually does not get enough fresh water from the sea through channels in the reef crown, and furthermore since the ground is covered with sand, the living conditions for corals are definitely less favorable here than at the reef crown.

Coral reefs constitute one of the most species-rich communities on earth. Only tropical rainforests and steppes or savannas (such as those in East Africa) are comparable.

Corals are the basic food for numerous animals like the well-known parrot fish, the infamous crown of thorns, and many multicolored nudibranchs and flat worms. The latter not only eat the coral. They do not digest the poisonous stinging cells but deposit them in their skin, creating an effective defensive weapon against predators. Bright red, black, and blue sponges bore their way into the coral, as do mussels or bristle worms with their patterned tentacle crowns.

Many stationary animals compete with the stone coral for space: the beautiful soft corals (**Fig. pages 48, 52–53, 62–63**) as well as other species of *Coelenterata* like the fire coral and sea anemones. (**Fig. pages 52–53**) The latter live in a very special symbiosis: anemone fish of the genus *Amphiprion* swim without danger between their stinging tentacles (**Fig. page 49–50**) because they develop a protective substance in their skin as a result of their constant contact with the sea anemones. They defend 'their' anemone with vehemence and are not afraid of the much bigger divers. The symbiosis between the cleaner wrasse or (**Fig. page 60**) the cleaner shrimp and their customers, including sometimes even dangerous predators like barracudas, is also well known. The little blue-, white-, and black-striped fish swims unconcerned in the toothy mouth of a two-meter-long barracuda. Even a diver may have the honour of getting his arms cleaned if he does not move.

Besides the many species of animals, from almost all branches of the animal kingdom, that are bound fast to the coral reef, there are countless other creatures that, although also found in other places, prefer to live in the reef. In the course of millions of years a network of numerous interwoven relationships among different species has developed in the coral reef and thereby created a habitat so rich in nutrients that even fish from the open sea such as sharks and barracudas come to find their prey. The primeval sea turtle (**Fig. page 56**) can be seen searching for food, and it is a unique experience to be circled by a huge manta ray, which shows little fear. (**Fig. page 56**)

This complex ecosystem cannot be described even close to completely. Every single time in our more than one hundred diving and snorkeling trips we discovered at least one lifeform we had not previously known – the coral reef will offer work for generations of scientists. Nevertheless, we want still to address some interesting and frequently discussed aspects.

The dangers of the reef are much discussed, especially among newcomers in Sinai. Some have to overcome considerable fear when entering the water with diving mask and snorkel for the first time at Sharm al-Sheikh or Ras Muhammad. They are primarily afraid of sharks, of which several species do exist in the Red Sea. The vantage rock of Ras Muhammad bears the name Shark Point with reason, as, at least a few years ago, sharks could frequently be observed there. In the Red Sea, the fear of sharks is quite unfounded if the diver observes certain rules and does not provoke them. Sharks are usually shy predators that flee from humans, which is why these magnificent predators are scarcely to be found nowadays at much-frequented reefs and diving places like Shark Point. Naturally, sharks are provoked by divers or snorklers carrying dead fish with them, but fishing is in any case prohibited in the reef areas of Egypt. The fish-blood in the water lures the nearby sharks without fail and may provoke in them a real rapacity. That accidents can happen under these circumstances is obvious and fishing divers have only themselves to blame. Furthermore, it is not very sensible to pull at the tail fins of sleeping nurse sharks or whitetip reef sharks. Although these animals are only 1.5 meters long they can be very dangerous in such situations. It is also dangerous to swim too far into the open sea, and harbor areas and ship routes especially should be avoided, because here sharks are used to eating ships' refuse on the surface of the water. A wriggling swimmer in such an area is an incitement for sharks. The only two accidents with sharks which we have heard of in the northern Red Sea happened under exactly such circumstances. A soldier, who wanted to swim from Sinai to the Isle of Tiran, was attacked by a mako shark in the area of the shipping lane. The same happened to a couple swimming next to a ship in the harbour of Eilat.

Divers and snorklers who stay calm in the water normally need not fear sharks. Instead they can be glad if they once get the rare opportunity to observe a slim reef shark, a ray-like angel shark, the strange hammerhead, or one of the various gray reef sharks.

The real dangers in the reef come from other creatures. Anyone familiar with the reef can easily avoid these dangers. The main rule is not to touch anything. On the one hand, living corals can be destroyed, and on the other, touching powerfully stinging fire corals can be very painful. Also, some of the brightly multicolored sponges, bristle worms, sea urchins, starfish, or cone shells, which can push out a mobile appendage with poison 'fangs,' sting strongly or are poisonous. Many fish have poisonous spines on their fins and opercula, as for example the lionfish, the fire lionfish, or the scorpion fish. (**Fig. pages 58, 61**) Rightly infamous are the extremely well camouflaged stonefish (**Fig. page 57**) whose poison almost always kills. One species which can be very unpleasant for divers is the titan triggerfish *(Balistoides viridescens)*. Normally, this rather large, 75-centimeter-long fellow keeps a respectful distance, but divers approaching too close to a male guarding eggs risk not only ugly holes in their diving suit but also severe injuries. Once an enraged titan triggerfish chased us more than two hundred meters along the coast and only our resolute defense with flippers and snorkels averted worse.

The magnificence of the Red Sea's coral reefs impressed visitors even in the last century. Famous zoologists like Rüppell, Ehrenberg, Brehm, Klunzinger, and Haeckel came to the Egyptian coast and to al-Tur in times when a journey to the Red Sea was a risky undertaking. Haeckel, who saw only the poor reefs at al-Tur from the boat, described this experience as the high point of his life. What would he have said if, equipped with a diving mask, he had seen the reefs at Ras Muhammad or in the Gulf of Aqaba, places that were unknown at that time? Even in 1939, an Englishman described the Gulf of Aqaba as a desolate sea, presumably without any corals.

The era of divers began in the Red Sea in 1949 at Port Sudan, when Hans Hass used his self-developed 'aqualung' for the first time. The German Hass and the Frenchman Jacques Yves Cousteau improved this technique very quickly, and their sensational reports and films from the reef soon caused others to dive with mask and diving equipment into this colorful world of underwater gardens. With the rapidly booming dive-tourism came the first dangers for the coral reef. A particularly bad habit was the use of underwater harpoons, which enabled divers to shoot whole reefs empty in some regions of the world. This is not surprising, since the reef fish are so tame that any child can shoot them. Fortunately, today this nonsense – once considered sport – is forbidden almost everywhere and is severely punished.

Other problems still exist for the reef and are made worse by the rapidly growing streams of vacationers to the coast of Sinai. Too many tourists carelessly walk not only over the reef top but also over the reef crown and thoughtlessly trample down whole corals. Also among numerous groups of underwater enthusiasts, there are too many poorly educated divers who touch everything with their hands or carelessly let whole corals tumble down the reef slopes when taking pictures. Allegedly, some underwater photographers even purposely break off corals in order to arrange them for the picture that later wins an award. Apart from the fact that every handhold on the corals destroys thousands of polyps, this activity can be extremely dangerous, as outlined above.

Meanwhile, the greatest threat to coral reefs is the increasing pollution of the sea. Garbage from ships and pollution with oil from illegal tank cleaning have already caused visible damage in places in the Red Sea. Touristic development, and the consequently increasing introduction of nutrient-rich organic sewage into the sea, may kill the reefs if every effort is not made to prevent it.

For the last few years, the main center for divers in Sinai has been the chaotically growing Sharm al-Sheikh, especially the hotel are of Naama Bay, located a few kilometers to the north. Other diving bases in the Gulf of Aqaba are at Dahab and Nuweiba. Nowadays, further diving bases have been set up in new and architecturally attractive hotel complexes along the entire coral coast from Ras Muhammad to Taba. Divers can rent the necessary equipment. In order to protect the coral reefs, diving is almost always done from boats, which are no longer allowed to anchor just anywhere in the reef, but only at special anchor buoys. Diving classes are offered everywhere. Among other things these classes teach the regulations for reef protection. In spite of some remaining abuses, a lot has been done during the last few years as Egyptian authorities as well as tourist suppliers have

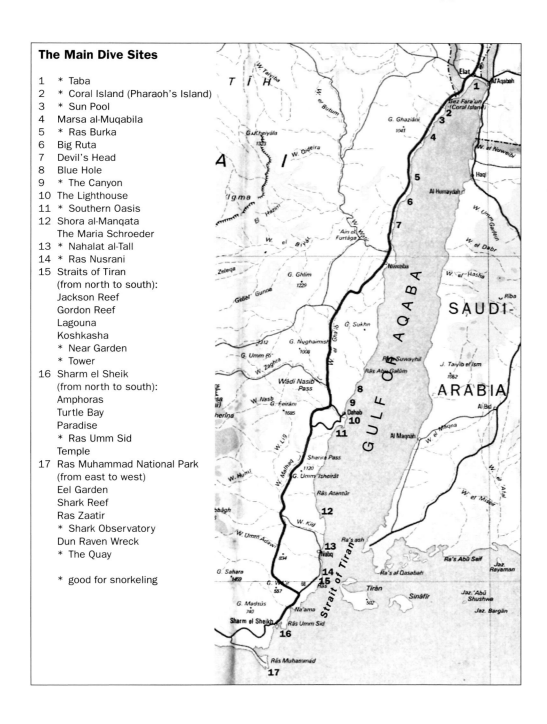

The Main Dive Sites

1   * Taba
2   * Coral Island (Pharaoh's Island)
3   * Sun Pool
4   Marsa al-Muqabila
5   * Ras Burka
6   Big Ruta
7   Devil's Head
8   Blue Hole
9   * The Canyon
10 The Lighthouse
11 * Southern Oasis
12 Shora al-Manqata
    The Maria Schroeder
13 * Nahalat al-Tall
14 * Ras Nusrani
15 Straits of Tiran
    (from north to south):
    Jackson Reef
    Gordon Reef
    Lagouna
    Koshkasha
    * Near Garden
    * Tower
16 Sharm el Sheik
    (from north to south):
    Amphoras
    Turtle Bay
    Paradise
    * Ras Umm Sid
    Temple
17 Ras Muhammad National Park
    (from east to west)
    Eel Garden
    Shark Reef
    Ras Zaatir
    * Shark Observatory
    Dun Raven Wreck
    * The Quay

    * good for snorkeling

Right:
The bearded boxthorn *(Lycium barbarum)* is a very rare plant that grows among the sand dunes in the vicinity of the Mitla Pass. Backlit by the rising sun, the little shrub looks like a burning bush.

recognized the coral reefs as an excellent source of foreign exchange that would be irretrievably lost if the reef were destroyed. Today, protective regulations exist and are enforced for the entire Egyptian coast of the Red Sea. Ras Muhammad has become a much better managed national park with firm, reasonable regulations. In addition to the very varied and always wonderful diving sites at Ras Muhammad, dives in the Straits of Tiran offer another supreme highlight, and there are other marvelous diving and snorkeling sites around Sharm al-Sheikh and along the gulf coast at Ras Nusrani, at a few places with unusual corals at the mouth of Wadi Kid near the little fishing village of Nabq (where the northernmost mangroves in the world grow), (**Fig. pages 46–47**) at the famous Canyon, and at the equally renowned Blue Hole north of Dahab.

At present, dive-tourism is the main pillar of tourism in Sinai. Older, and still of great importance, are the tours to St. Catherine's Monastery in the heart of the peninsula. A recent independent development is desert tourism, which as a supplement to the experience of the Red Sea focuses on the fascinating desert landscape as the main attraction: tourists drive in cross-country vehicles through the Wadi Arada, ride on camelback to the Rainbow Canyon (**Fig. page 31**) and to Ain Umm Ahmad, hike in wadis among the highest Sinai mountains, guided by Bedouin, or climb Mount Sinai and Gabal Katrin.

One can only hope that this kind of tourism will not grow to the extent that it destroys the very special attractions of Sinai: the unmatched silence and loneliness of a singular landscape hard by the colorful magic of the Red Seas coral gardens.

The Timna civilization flourished around 3800–2650 BC. The *nawamis* (above and right) are tombs that today lie lost in an uninhabitable desert. Their surprisingly good condition shows how carefully they were built. The word *nawamis* (sing. *namusiya*) comes from a root referring to 'mosquito.' According to a biblical legend, the *nawamis* were built for protection against a plague of mosquito. In fact, the *nawamis* are much older, and excavations verify their function as tombs at the end of the first Timna period. Burial objects such as pearls from the shells of the spider conch, copper needles, bangles, a few flint tools, rolled copper wire, and some fragments of ceramics have been found in *nawamis*. After burial, the tomb was filled with earth, then the roof was closed with stone slabs.

Opposite :
On the mountain above the turquoise mines, the ancient Egyptians built the Hathor Temple of Serabit al-Khadim, whose name means 'steles of serving.' Although many of the steles have been broken, the ruins still offer an impressive sight (left, above and below). The royal cartouche of Sahure (left) verifies that the pharaohs mined copper in Sinai as early as the Fifth Dynasty.

Above:
The remains of the ancient bishops' see of Pharan are being uncovered in the course of the ongoing excavations in Wadi Feiran.

Right:
Numerous rock pictures can be found in the sandstone area of Sinai. Most of them can be dated to the time of the Nabataeans. Collections of such rock pictures mark stopping-places on ancient trade routes. Inscriptions and pictures have also been made in other periods up to the present day.

Mount Sinai boasts numerous places with an ancient religious tradition. A path from St. Catherine's Monastery leads up several thousand steps directly to the peak. The steps were made by a monk to fulfil a vow. The steep stairway is spanned by two stone arches, the Arch of St. Stephanos (above) and the Arch of Faith. In the sixth century the hermit Stephanos kept watch that no unworthy person climbed up Mount Sinai and so he heard the pilgrims' confession at the arch. The skeleton of Stephanos is wrapped up in a monk's cassock and still sits as a porter in the monastery's charnel house. From the Arch of Faith the believer had to climb up the mountain on bare feet. On a plateau below the peak, near an ancient cypress and a spring, are two small chapels, one consecrated to Moses, the other to Elijah.

Left:
A chapel and a mosque stand on Mount Sinai. The chapel was built from the remains of a church dating from 530 that itself stood on the foundations of an older chapel built in 363.

Left:
Surrounded by the impressive backdrop of the highest granite mountains in Sinai, St. Catherine's Monastery stands like a sturdy fortress at the end of the valley of Wadi Deir. Beside the monastery's basilica with

its filigree belltower is the white minaret of the mosque. Directly behind the monastery the steep climb to Mount Sinai over the 'Way of Steps' begins.

Above:
The brilliant, sumptuously decorated interior of the basilica contrasts stunningly with the austere exterior of St. Catherine's Monastery.

Following pages:
The view from Mount Sinai at sunrise reveals an immense mountain landscape with its rough and grandiose beauty in the highest and oldest part of Sinai.

Above:
On an imposing and strongly fissured mountain in Wadi Sidr, Salah al-Din had the fortress of Qal'at al-Gundi ('Soldier's Citadel') built around 1180 AD in order to protect Egypt against Crusaders from Palestine.
The entrance arch (left), built without mortar, is interesting evidence of Islamic stuctural engineering.

Right:
Coral Island, at the end of the Gulf of Aqaba (above), has a turbulent history. As an outpost, it protected the harbor of Eilat/Aqaba, the ancient Aila, with a citadel. The fortress, restored with much use of cement, goes back to Salah al-Din. Earlier the island was in the possession of the Crusaders for a short time.

Below right:
The mausoleum of Nabi Saleh stands in the middle of a Bedouin cemetery. Along the road to the St. Catherine's Monastery, where the track branches off to the Blue Mountains, lies the tomb of this most important Bedouin saint. Nabi Saleh is honored beyond Sinai: he is supposed to have ascended to heaven with his camel not only from Mount Sinai but also from Mecca, Cairo, and Damascus, and there are two other places in the Middle East where he is supposed to be buried.

As everywhere else, corrugated iron, plastic, and concrete have found their way to Bedouin settlements (left: a village in southern Sinai), and the camel has been replaced by the pickup.

The Bedouin tent (above and right) also called the 'house of hair,' will soon be part of the past. It is an unwritten but strictly followed law that a tent tied up and hanging in a tree should not be stolen.

Following pages:
When we met this Bedouin (left) from the area of al-Arish in northern Sinai he was collecting bazooka shells in the desert. These shells are dangerous remnants of the last Egyptian-Israeli wars. The pictures on the right show Bedouin women in traditional dresses. The face veil or *burqa'* shows the status and wealth of a woman. The *burqa'* of the Bedouin woman from northern Sinai (below left) is decorated with valuable coins.

Above:
A good riding-camel is still the pride of a wealthy Bedouin. Every good camel has a richly embellished saddle. In the age of tourism, the camel has new meaning as a source of income. Camel-tours from Sharm al-Sheikh or Nuweiba to the mountains are justifiably becoming more and more popular. Recently, Bedouin have organized camel races in picturesque wadis as a further tourist attraction. On such occasions, they also show beautiful Arabian horses.

Right:
Goats are extremely adaptable domestic animals that find food in the desert even in places where other animals would have starved or died of thirst long ago.

Left:
The faces of these village children from the area of al-Arish are a reflection of the people who, in the course of a long history, have used the Way of Horus as passage route through northern Sinai.

Above:
At Bedouin social gatherings, men and women usually sit in separate groups. The tea-drinking ceremony is always important and hospitality is a holy tradition that requires that even enemies be protected when they have been taken in as guests.

Left:
In northern Sinai tradition and modernity collide even in agriculture. Next to progressive cultivation methods like plastic tunnels, some Bedouin work with ancient plows made of wood or loosen the soil with heavy iron hoes.
Above:
Under the protection of palm groves near al-Arish grain is planted extensively.

Following page:
In such an inhospitable mountain desert the idea of the garden of paradise must have originated in ancient times (above). In places where a little water from the mountains collects in the rough gravel of the wadis, delicious pomegranates (below left), grapes (below right), peaches (right), and other tasty fruits grow. Among the trees, the air is perfumed by all the herbs of the East.

Above left:
A street café in al-Arish. Holiday camps are beginning to characterize the coastal landscape. When modern hotels take up traditional elements of the country, they become especially attractive to tourists. Every evening the Bedouin tent in front of this white hotel in Sharm al-Sheikh is full of people.

Above:
Tourist dreams are realized even by guests from the Arabian Peninsula. The crystal-clear water invites even beginners to snorkel.

Following pages:
The aerial photograph shows Naama Bay at Sharm al-Sheikh. This bay quickly became the tourist center of South Sinai.

Above:
In 1980 a French artist spread thirteen tons of blue paint over rocks in Wadi Nafakh to make the so-called Blue Mountains in order to "add the human dimension to the natural dimension." The result is debatable. The colors, which were supposed to last at least one hundred years, have already started to flake off.

Above right:
This picture shows the effects of oil-drilling on the Gulf of Suez. The African coast can seldom be seen so clearly in the background.

Below right:
A lonely remnant of manganese mining at Umm Bugma. The manganese deposits, often not very productive, are located in the same area as the copper deposits that were exploited by the ancient Egyptians.

History

From the Stone Age to the October War

Autumn 1990: The broad and sandy wadi with only a few isolated acacias narrows and leads to the right into the mountains. We climb straight ahead up a small path, scarcely wider than a goat track. Between two not-so-high mountain ridges the path reaches a pass, suddenly giving a wonderful view of the precipitous peaks of the Serbal chain. A moment later, I pick up a stone and discover in my hand a hand ax of flint. (**Fig. page 82**) A barely visible track in a wild, lonely landscape turns out to be an ancient pass, which was obviously used in the Stone Age. A few meters farther on, primitive pictures of three ibexes, scratched into the rock at the wayside a long time ago confirm the first impression.

This was not the first time we had found traces of history during our Sinai travels. In some places Sinai is strewn with historical relics, which reveal themselves to those who have learned to look more closely: rock paintings, old ruins, flint arrowheads, deserted copper and turquoise mines, pharaonic inscriptions, barrows, stone heaps, 'desert dragons,' granite pillars, and of course St. Catherine's Monastery with its art treasures from many centuries – all bear witness to a history reaching back to the beginnings of humankind. Far less pleasant are the remnants of recent history: burned-out tanks, cannons shot to pieces, barbed wire, and frequently unmarked minefields are sad relics of Israeli-Egyptian wars.

The profusion of signs of historical happenings in an appearently empty desert landscape is astonishing only at first glance. The location between the ancient and present powers of Egypt and Palestine, between Africa and Asia is once again a decisive factor.

For a long time, historians regarded Sinai only as a stage for biblical Christian events and as a through-route for mercenaries, traders, pilgrims, and nomads. The mining activities of ancient Egyptians have also left plainly visible traces. The realization that the peninsula was not just the playground of neighboring regions or the territory of a few rapacious nomads was the contribution of Beno Rothenberg. In 1956 he began archaeological investigations in Sinai, but not until 1967 was a team under his leadership able to begin systematic recording by modern methods. His research work verified for the first time that Sinai not only was populated since primeval times but also twice experienced the development of its own indigenous civilizations.

Stone Age

Stone Age finds such as flint tools are not rare in Sinai. But for the non-expert they are difficult to classify as, according to Rothenberg, this period covers the almost inconceivable range of time from 700,000 to 4,500 years BC. This huge span is divided according certain criteria and characteristics

Left:
The copper mines in Wadi Kharig. One of the mines that provided ancient Egypt with this important resource was located here. A slag heap can still be seen in the foreground.

of finds and find locations into several epochs, which still cover scarcely conceivable periods of time. Historically interpretable finds discovered at Gabal Maghara date from the early Paleozoic. Every time the climate became more humid (as happened about 35,000 and 7000 years ago), settlements grew up at the foot of the mountains in the Tih desert. In dry periods, however, the area was deserted.

Significant connections between the inhabitants of Sinai and settlers on the Arabian Peninsula are discernable in the Neolithic Age. Rothenberg excavated wall tombs up to eighty meters long and 1.5 meters wide and neolithic places of worship like those in eastern Arabia. Perhaps the most important result of these excavations was the recognition that even as far back as the Stone Age humans followed the water and the paths they still use through the desert today. The dangerous, waterless desert has been the center of the Tih Plateau ever since the beginning of human memory, and only on the slopes of the mountains have humans been able to settle from time to time. On the other hand, the edges of the Tih Fault, which abound in water, and the basement complex in the south, have always permitted human settlement. First, only watering-places, grazing land, and sites with flint attracted humans; later also turquoise and copper deposits. The history of settlement in Sinai was thus dictated by geological and geographical conditions right from the beginning.

Eilat Culture

The first evidently autonomous development of civilization in Sinai, about 4500–3800 BC, was named the Eilat Culture by Rothenberg. The humans of this early copper epoch probably immigrated from the Arabian Peninsula. According to their artifacts, they were seminomads who lived in primitive round, stone walls and made their living mainly as shepherds and flint workers, but sickle blades and flint axes indicate the beginnings of a primitive agriculture.

Timna Culture

Named after the first place such artifacts were found in the Timna Valley, this period from about 3800 to 2650 BC witnessed the development of the most important indigenous civilization in Sinai. The Timna people were also seminomadic. Around their huts and tents they built round walls of boulders into which they drove their livestock at night. Fireplaces discovered during excavations seem to be the remains of protected farmsteads. The Timna people distinguished themselves by considerable cultural achievements. In addition to a more advanced flint technique they had their own ceramics, mined copper, and used copper tools. Moreover, they developed their own distinctive architecture and built a relatively large settlement that could be called a city.

With their stone buildings the Timna people created sights that tourists can still look at with astonishment today. The *nawamis* (sing. *namusiya*) (**Fig. pages 82–83**) are round houses built of carefully laid, unworked stone slabs, with a small, often square entrance toward the west. Exceptional in this construction is the stratification of a double wall that made it possible to lay a flat, round, stone roof from the sides to the middle. Some of these

more than five-thousand-year-old roofs are still intact. The very small entrances suggest that the *nawamis* were not dwellings but tombs, reminiscent
of ancient Egyptian tombs in their west-facing aspect. Burial objects made
of copper point to close relations with the ancient pre-pharaonic Egypt. The
most famous *nawamis* are thirty well-preserved tombs discovered by Rothenberg not far from the oasis Ain Hudra. Shortly before sunset, this collection
of ancient stone buildings in the lonely, bizarre desert landscape presents a
moving view. The *nawamis* are also associated with biblical history. Legend
says that on their way through the desert, some hungry Israelites who had
died of a surfeit of quails sent by God, were buried in *nawamis*. It is certain
that the *nawamis* were used as tombs several times over.

The so-called 'desert dragons' are ancient traps for gazelles that probably date from the Timna period as well. These traps consist of remains of
very long stone walls that come together at acute angles. The gazelles were
driven into the narrow ends in order to kill them. Following the Timna
people, the Bedouin used these traps until a few years ago. Today, the
desert dragons have often been dismantled or covered with sand and are
therefore hard to see.

West of Gabal Budhiya, not too far from Ras Sidr, Rothenberg discovered a remarkable field of ruins. Excavations exposed the remains of a surprisingly large settlement with a central square and cult buildings unique to
Sinai. This settlement can be described as a city. Artifacts from this excava-
tion once again indicate lively trade relations between Timna and Egypt.

Ancient Egypt

The establishment of the Egyptian empire by pharaohs of the First Dynasty
who came from Upper Egypt about 3000 BC had a serious impact on the
Timna civilization. During the unification of the empire, the new rulers from
Upper Egypt not only conquered Lower Egypt in several campaigns but
also repeatedly celebrated victories over Asians in their pictorial records.
In all probability these Asians were Timna people. An important confirma-
tion of this is a commemorative inscription of Snofru found on a rock face
next to the turquoise mines of Maghara. Snofru was one of the most important rulers of the Fourth Dynasty and is regarded as the conqueror of Sinai.
The Egyptologist Flinders Petrie had these and other similar inscriptions
chiseled out of Sinai's rocks and transported by camel and ship to Cairo in
order to save them from destruction. Today most of them are in the Egyptian
Museum in Cairo.

Although the Egyptian occupation of Sinai did not last long, the Timna
people remained under the pharaohs' hegemony, and their culture gradually died out. Egyptian influence in Sinai covers (including interruptions) the
period from 2900 to 526 BC. During this whole period the peninsula was
important to the Egyptians mainly because the important trade and military
road to Palastine ran along the Mediterranean coast. Called the Way of
Horus, it was used by the Egyptian military for their campaigns of conquest.
In the opposite direction, Asians such as the Amoritic shepherd warriors or
the Hyksos penetrated into Egypt in several waves of immigration, causing
first the Old and then later the Middle kingdoms to collapse.

The turquoise and copper mines of Timna were located in southern
Sinai. The pharaohs sent mining expeditions here whenever necessary and

A broken stele in the temple of Serabit al-Khadim shows the hieroglyphic inscription of part of an accounting record. Every bow-mark, for example, stands for the number ten.

had first the Timna people work for them and later their local successors, under Egyptian leadership and for Egyptian benefit. Nevertheless, there are some signs that indicate that there must have been some kind of contract between the Egyptians and the inhabitants of Sinai, who did not work as slaves. The remains of this extensive mining activity can still be seen. Besides rock pictures, inscriptions and steles of Pharaohs, there are mine entrances, slag heaps, remains of kilns, foundation walls of primitive houses, fortified work camps, mouthpieces of burning-nozzles, and smelting clinker.

The ruins of the temple of Serabit al-Khadim from the Twelfth Dynasty lie in a wonderful location with a view of the Tih Fault. Flinders Petrie carried out the first scientific investigations here. The temple was consecrated to the Egyptian goddess Hathor and to the local god Sopdu, ruler of the east. This shows that Egyptian and local miners prayed and made their sacrifices in the same temple. Not far away are the copper mines of Bir Nasib with their large slag heaps and inscriptions of Amenemhat III, and mines in Wadi Kharig with inscriptions of Sahure and a stele of Sesostris I. (**Fig. page 112**) Other important copper mines are located in Wadi Baba, Wadi Shellal, Wadi Riqeita, and north of Eilat. The last great copper pharaoh was Ramses III (ca. 1200–1168 BC), who was also one of the most powerful pharaohs of the New Kingdom. Afterward, Egyptian influence in Sinai diminished without interruption until 526 BC, when the Persian conquest of the pharaohs' empire extinguished it completely.

The Nabataeans

The importance of the Nabataeans in Sinai's history was overlooked for a long time. In the third or fourth century BC they founded an empire in the area of their capital Petra in Jordan that during its peak extended over northwestern Saudi Arabia and the Negev. The Nabataeans were Hellenistically-influenced Arabs and extremely successful traders. They left conspicuous traces in Sinai: rock paintings and inscriptions decorate countless boulders and rock walls, especially in the region of the sandstone belt. Collections of such rock paintings, for example in Wadi Maktab, mark the stopping-places along the ancient trade routes. Inscriptions in Bir Nasib verify that the Nabataeans continued copper mining until the Roman period. Their wealth provoked Roman greed and was the main reason for the campaign of conquest in 106 BC. The Nabataeans apparently remained active traders, though, as their rock inscriptions can be dated into Byzantine time.

Protosinaitic Script

Together with ancient Egyptian and younger Nabataean inscriptions, on rocks as well as in the temple ruins of Serabit al-Khadim can be seen what appear to be arbitrarily scribbled characters that upon closer examination prove to be hieroglyphs. What excited linguists soon after the discovery of these characters was the realization that here was an alphabetic script consisting only of consonants. Today, it is acknowledged that this so-called protosinaitic script was a preliminary stage in the development of the alphabetic scripts of the Hebrews, Aramaeans, and Phoenicians. From the Phoenicians the Greeks derived their script, which was the basis for our Latin alphabet. The protosinaitic script was presumably used by Canaani-

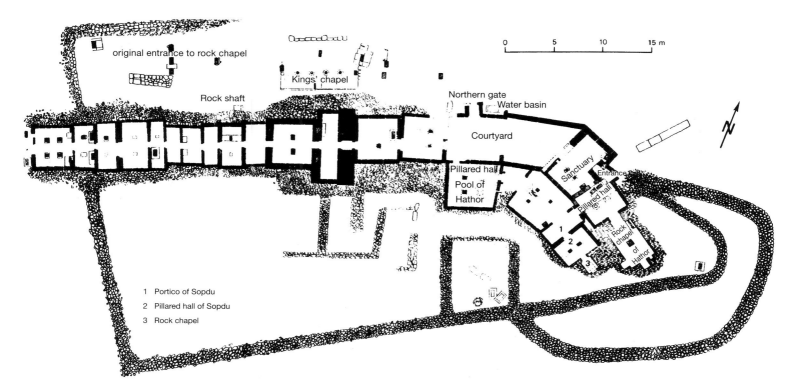

original entrance to rock chapel

Kings' chapel

Rock shaft

Northern gate
Water basin

Courtyard

Sanctuary
Entrance

Pillared hall
Pool of Hathor

Pillared hall

1
2
Rock chapel of Hathor
3

1 Portico of Sopdu
2 Pillared hall of Sopdu
3 Rock chapel

0   5   10   15 m

tic miners and is therefore not of Nabataean origin. Sinai thus holds an archaeological find of the greatest significance for human civilization.

History of Religion in Sinai

For Jews, Christians, and Muslims Sinai is holy land and inseparably bound to their religious traditions. Whoever has been in Sinai's mountains knows that this is not a historical coincidence but partly a contribution of the Sinai landscape. The feeling of boundless loneliness in such a barren but also overwhelming landscape makes earthly things appear unimportant and provides room for thoughts about the beginning and end of the world.

It cannot be determined exactly when the patriarch Abraham came from Ur in Mesopotamia to Sinai and to the region of the present-day Suez Canal. But it was probably during the Twelfth Dynasty, which would mean that Sinai's religious tradition reaches back to almost two thousand years before Christ.

It is certain that Israelite tribes came to Sinai in several waves of immigration only much later, during the Second Intermediate Period (1785–1580 BC). They lived as seminomads in western Sinai and at the edge of Lower Egypt. It was probably from this area that Joseph came, who the Bible tells us rose to become the pharaoh's adviser.

Moses was probably born in the early Ramesside period (about 1300 BC). As a foundling he grew up in the pharaoh's court. He must have known the Sinai desert well before he was able to lead the exodus of the Israelites. Years earlier he had fled from the pharaoh after a disagreement to the Midianites in Sinai, where he married the daughter of the priest and looked after the herds of his father-in-law. There he also experienced the appearance of the burning bush. Abraham and Moses belong to the foundations of Judaism, Christianity, and Islam.

The Israelites' exodus out of Egypt probably took place during the rule of the Ramses II, at the latest during the rule of his successor Merenptah, so approximately between 1298 and 1230 BC. The exodus through the desert and the revelation in Sinai are basic elements of Old Testament

Simplified ground plan of Serabit al-Khadim.
The British Egyptologist Sir Flinders Petrie started the first archaeological investigations in 1905. Earlier Sinai researchers include the Swiss Johann L. Burckhardt who traveled as 'Sheikh Ibrahim Ibn Abdullah' through the Near East in 1816, then the German zoologist Eduard Rüppell from 1822 to 1831, the French nobleman Léon de Laborde in 1830, and the Scottish painter David Roberts in 1839.

The rock picture of the seven-branched candlestick, the Jewish Menorah, in Wadi Umm Sideira testifies to Jewish pilgrims in eastern Sinai. Rothenberg deciphered the Latin inscription written across the candlestick as *victoria augusti Caesaris* ('victory of the noble Caesar').

faith. The historical events are still disputed, which is not surprising since wandering groups of nomads – for such were the tribes of Israel at this time-leave few historically readable traces. Thus even those places in Sinai with names referring to Moses – Uyun Musa ('Springs of Moses') south of al-Shatt, Hammam Sayyidna Musa ('Bath of Our Lord Moses') near al-Tur, and Gabal Musa ('Mount Moses': Mount Sinai) are not reliably historical sites. It is also uncertain whether Moses and his people took a northern route along the Mediterranean coast or the southern one through Wadi Feiran. On the other hand, Rothenberg's investigations made it clear that the Amalekites, an old desert tribe and the Israelites' traditional archenemies, had settled in the Negev mountains and in northeastern Sinai around Kadesh (today Quseima) even before Abraham's time.

Christian settlement in Sinai began in the third and fourth centuries AD. Hermits and early Christian pilgrims who wanted to settle down in proximity to the biblical places first came from the Coptic desert monasteries of Upper Egypt and the Eastern Desert. Christian settlements arose in al-Tur, the ancient Raithou (which some authors misplace in Wadi Garandel), and in Wadi Feiran. Around Mount Sinai there were numerous hermitages and monastic colonies. Very soon they were raided by Arab Saracens and Nubian Blemyes. In the raids the nomads killed many hermits and monks, who went down in history as martyrs. The 'Garden' and the 'Monastery of Forty Martyrs' still exist today in Wadi Leiga between Mount Sinai and Gabal Katrin. The Saracen queen Mavia converted to Christianity and appointed a converted Saracen monk named Moses first bishop of Pharan, and the Feiran Oasis became the bishop's see.

Aetheria, the nun who made an extremely arduous pilgrimage to the holy places from 393 to 396 AD, gives a very vivid and historically valuable description of the early Christian situation in Sinai. Her records describe monastic life at the Holy Bush and on Mount Sinai long before St. Catherine's Monastery was built.

The attacks on the monks by the surrounding nomads did not end, so in response to to the monks' pleading the emperor Justinian had a monasterial fortress built between 548 and 565 AD. (**Fig. pages 88–89**) Justinian's master builder Stephanus was beheaded after finishing his work because he had chosen for strategic reasons to build at the place of the legendary Burning Bush at the end of Wadi Deir, rather than on a mountaintop as the emperor had wished. The monastery was originally consecrated to the Virgin Mary, but the ever-increasing veneration of St. Catherine in the late Middle Ages led the monks to choose her as their patron saint. Only legends tell of the life and death of Catherine of Alexandria. The legends say she was an aristocratic and educated virgin who, as a Christian, denounced the dissipated lifestyle of the Roman emperor. As fifty of his learned philosophers converted to Christianity during debate with her, the emperor became furious and incarcerated her. After a failed attempt to execute her, the emperor had her beheaded with an instrument of torture. Angels took Catherine's body up to the mountain that since bears her name. Furthermore, the legend says that since some partridges followed the angels, God made a spring bubble up for them on the mountaintop, since known as Bir al-Shumar ('Partridge Spring').

The mighty fortress – with its cypress-adorned garden, and surrounded by the red granite peaks of the highest Sinai mountains – is a fascinating sight, and it is the location of simultaneously continuous and changing history. The changing times are directly visible in the monastery, since a mosque from the time of the Fatimids (909 – 1171 AD) stands right next to the Christian basilica. And the continuity can be seen in the fact that the basilica is the oldest Christian church in the world, in which the liturgy has been read and chanted for fifteen hundred years without interruption.

Soon after its foundation, the monastery was threatened several times by Muslim warriors in the seventh century. First, the monastery was saved by a letter of protection that the Prophet Muhammad himself allegedly signed for the monastery. Although historians have doubts about the authenticity of this letter, it obviously served its purpose many times. The construction of a mosque in the interior of the monastery is also ascribed to a stratagem of the monks. A former guest house from the sixth century was rebuilt in the twelfth century as the mosque; in the southern walls they set niches to mark its orientation toward Mecca. The interior of the mosque is furnished with a valuable pulpit and other precious works of art from the Fatimid period. Today this mosque is one of only three almost intact mosques preserved from the Fatimid period.

Numerous stonemasons' signs incorporating Christian symbolism from the sixth century can be seen on the outside wall of St. Catherine's Monastery.

The end of the monastery's golden age began in the eleventh century and by the eighteenth century, the monks had been forced out at least eight times. Only in 1800, during his Egyptian campaign, did Napoleon guarantee the monastery's attested rights. As an enclave of Greek Orthodox Christianity, the monastery was placed then in the care of the Russian tsar. Today, the monastery is independent within the Greek Orthodox Church. Most of the monks come from Greece and live an ascetic life, which today is increasingly disturbed by growing tourism. Unfortunately, this also effects Mount Sinai, which threatens to become a rubbish dump and at times stinks like a latrine.

Not only its religious significance but also its unique art treasures make St. Catherine's Monastery rightly famous. The interior of the basilica, (**Fig. page 89**) with its consistent architectural and artistic decoration, leaves a memorable impression. The mosaic on the vault, depicting the transfiguration of Christ, belongs to the most important Byzantine mosaics, and the icon collection, with about two thousand items – among them some very rare wax icons from the sixth and seventh centuries – is especially interesting for art enthusiasts. The library contains invaluable manuscripts from the early Christian era. Of special importance is the Codex Sinaiticus from the fourth century.

Sinai as a Region of Transit

Although Sinai does have its own history of settlement and civilisation, for much of the time from the Stone Age until today the peninsula has served primarily as a transit corridor between Egypt and Palestine and between the empires of Africa and Asia. The Sinai desert was for long stretches of time a nearly deserted and economically insignificant place that was left to roving nomadic Bedouin. The main way was and is still the route along the Mediterranean Sea, since there the water supply is certain and travel is not obstructed by mountains. Apart from the coastal route, there are three other routes long of great importance: the desert track from Ismailia to Nizana; the Islamic pilgrimage routes from Suez to Eilat, Darb al-Hagg and

Darb al-Shawi; and the southern route from Suez through Wadi Feiran, which finally leads north again to Eilat and provided access to the copper and turquoise mines. On these routes, where Stone Age shepherds and hunters once wandered from one watering place to another, marched pharaonic armies and their Asiatic opponents. The Romans turned them into highways, and Islamic troops rode along them on their conquering assault on North Africa. After North Africa's conversion to Islam, the Darb al-Hagg was made into a splendid road for religious pilgrims to Mecca. Those times are attested to by the fortress Qal'at al-Gundi, built by Saladin (**Fig. page 92**) in Wadi Sidr; the ruins of the caravansary in Nakhl, unfortunately destroyed in the war in 1956; and the 180-meter-long rocky passage of Aqabat al-Urqub east of al-Thamad with its monumental inscriptions from the Mamluk period. The fortress on the island Gaziret al-Fara'un in the Gulf of Aqaba built to protect the harbour of Eilat is evidence of this Islamic pilgrim tradition as well. The recently reconstructed fortress stands on the ruins of a fortress Salah al-Din had built about 1115 AD. A crusader fortress stood there previously. The present name of Pharaoh's Island is rather misleading, and it is often known as Coral Island. (**Fig. page 93**)

The Crusaders marched through Sinai five times. Then came the Turkish conquerors, and even Napoleon's troops used the Sinai roads. After Egyptian independence, the Tih desert was a theater for the tank battles between Israel and Egypt, and once again the ancient desert routes were used as military highways. With the October War in 1973 this historical phase ended for the time being, and Israeli-occupied Sinai was returned to Egypt in 1982 according to the Camp David Agreement.

As the most recent history has shown in the Gulf War, Sinai's tradition as a transit region is obviously not over. In the fall of 1990, a strange picture presented itself: a stream of luxury limousines with Kuwaiti licence plates and roofs piled so high with suitcases, boxes, and crates that the worst fear was for the vehicles' axles and springs. On the road to Suez, the old pigrimage route of Darb al-Hagg, vehicle followed vehicle in an seemingly endless convoy headed toward Cairo and away from Saddam Hussein's invading troops.

The Egyptian government forces the pace of Sinai's economic and touristic development forward. The shock of the Israeli occupation has shaken the land awake. Old desert tracks have been turned into modern asphalt highways. Meanwhile, it is to be feared that too much is being done, as for instance in the destruction of the delightful Wadi Watir caused by construction of a rather unnecessary road. And if plans to construct a bridge from Saudi Arabia to Ras Nusrani over the Island and the Straits of Tiran should be realized, it would be a terrible intrusion in the landscape of the entire southern Sinai.

Be that as it may, all efforts aim at taking final possession of Sinai. Modern Egypt completes thereby the old tradition of the ancient Egyptians, who always saw Sinai as a sphere of influence that could be utilized when required but never really considered Egyptian territory.

In the very recent past, in October 1993, history was made again in Sinai. The hotel in Taba, close to Eilat on the Gulf of Aqaba and returned to Egypt only in 1989, was the venue for the Palestinian-Israeli peace conference, at which the autonomy agreement for Gaza and Jericho was to be realized. Egypt as host had taken on the patronage of these negotiations.

People

Shaped by the Desert

Desert plants and animals had to become specialists in order to survive under the hard conditions of Sinai's extreme environment. In a long adaptation process they have reshaped their bodies, developed their organs, and changed their metabolism in order to cope with heat and cold, aridity and salt content, wind and moving sand all at the same time. The price that had to be paid for successful adaptation is that desert plants and most desert animals can exist only in the desert. Things are quite different for human inhabitants of the desert. The desert environment caused no organic or physical changes in humans. It is a fact that humans are able to survive under so many different environmental conditions only because we are naturally so unspecialized.

Nevertheless, humans cannot permanently settle in the desert without any adaptation. As desert inhabitants they show behavior, use knowledge, and develop survival strategies that are useful solely in the desert. Human adaptation shows itself in the way people's whole lives are suffused and shaped by the hard nature of the environment.

Sinai's real desert inhabitants are the Bedouin who wander through the wild land as nomads and seminomads. Nowadays, the Bedouin are not the only inhabitants of the peninsula, and under the increasing influence of foreign neighbors and modern development quite a number of them are giving up their traditional way of life in the desert.

Reliable population figures for Sinai are difficult to obtain. Apart from the approximately one hundred thousand Bedouin, a large number of Egyptian soldiers live mostly in the north of the peninsula in military camps almost cut off from other inhabitants. Other Egyptians work in Sinai in the oil industry, in mines, in agricultural projects, and in the vigorously growing tourist industry. These Egyptian workers live primarily in coastal towns. Their total number is estimated to be about fifty thousand. In addition, a small group of immigrants from all over the world live in Sinai and work as qualified employees in the tourism and oil industries. The population structure could change totally, however, if the plans of former president Sadat are realized. In order to ease the situation in Cairo and the Nile Delta, plans were made to induce five million Egyptians to settle in Sinai's desert.

Sinai Bedouin are primarily descendants of those Arabic immigrants who came to Sinai in waves over a millenium in the course of the expansion of Islam. Appearently no direct descendants of the original inhabitants of Sinai survive, and even the Nabataeans seem to have vanished without trace. On the Mediterranean coast, especially around al-Arish, lives a very mixed population reflecting the varied history of Sinai. (**Fig. pages 100–101**)

The origin of the Bedouin is set out in the Old Testament: 'real' Bedouin regard Ismail, the son of Abraham, as their ancestor. The various tribes thus go back to the twelve sons of Ismail. The more direct the genealogy, the more distinguished is the tribe. The detailed exposition of close and distant relatives is still one of the most important topics of conversation for Bedouin. Embroidered with numerous little anecdotes, the ancestral line is memorized back to the tenth or twelfth generation.

A notable exception is the Gabaliya tribe from Mount Sinai. Their Christian ancestors originally came from Romania and from the area around Alexandria and were recruited by the emperor Justinian in the sixth century to build and protect St. Catherine's Monastery. As early as the seventh century the majority of these people converted to Islam, but other Bedouin still despise them as "Monastery Bedouin." Their place of worship is the small mosque inside St. Catherine's Monastery. The last Christian Gabaliya Bedouin is said to have died in the middle of the eighteenth century. Christian elements can be found, though, in the religious life of the Gabaliya Bedouin even today. On God's mountain they celebrate a feast for the patriarch Moses and sacrifice goats and sheep. They honor Christian saints, among them especially St. Catherine and St. George. Their supreme judge is the archbishop of the monastery.

The term 'Bedouin' is not a name for a specific people but characterizes a way of life. The Arabic word *badawi* means 'desert inhabitant.' Bedouin also like to call themselves 'Arab' to differentiate themselves from the fellaheen, the despised farmers of the Nile Valley. Bedouin were originally camel-breeders and nomads. The Bedouin's behaviour is so well suited to this desert-adapted mammal, strictly not a camel but a dromedary, that together they are able to survive with no problems in even the driest terrain. The Bedouin's life cycle is exclusively determined by the dromedary's needs. In order to reach their summer and winter pastures, Bedouin travel some hundred kilometers per year through the desert. Highly esteemed, the camel earns the title 'uncle'; it serves as a means of payment, for example for the bride-price, and in cases of blood feud one party can buy itself out by giving camels to the other party. These camels are called 'sleep camels' because they guarantee good sleep to the five generations on which the blood feud could be carried out, from the murderer's grandfather down to his grandsons.

Traveling around like the Bedouin, in the Tih desert for example, can still be fatal for the inexperienced visitor, especially since orientation in the desert is made difficult by the monotonous landscape. Only those with practiced eyes can find the often ancient trails. It is not enough to know the location of wells and watering-places. It is also necessary to be able to evaluate their present condition, as the water level can vary greatly as a result of dry periods or excessive use. For the Bedouin's livestock it is extremely important that the pastures really are green when they arrive, since the way to another pasture may be too long for the exhausted animals. Using a mixture of acute observation of nature, acquaintance with the local area, handed-down knowledge, and their own experiences, the desert nomads are able to cope with these and other problems. Their abilities determine hunting success as well. A Bedouin knows very well whether a plant is edible, has healing powers, is poisonous, or intoxicates like a drug.

Nomads like these camel-breeders are dying out in Sinai as in North Africa and Asia as well. All countries bordering on desert try to stop the uncontrolled movement of the allegedly thieving hordes – by increased military presence, by opening up the desert, and by appropriation of land.

Political borders to which Bedouin hardly paid attention in earlier times are ever more strictly guarded and so interrupt the old trails. Political programs and projects to settle Bedouin only contribute to the restriction of the Bedouin's freedom of movement.

This general tendency is very advanced in Sinai, where today the majority of Bedouin live in every possible transitional stage of permanent settlement. Most Sinai Bedouin live as seminomads breeding small animals like goats and sheep. In addition, in places with more water, such as oases and mountain wadis, they practice a rather meager agriculture. Hunting plays a smaller, ever-diminishing role, since after the decimation of most of the big game species it is limited to birds and smaller animals.

Many Bedouin live, at least in certain seasons, in stone houses or huts of wood, cardboard, corrugated iron, and plastic. The famous tent of goat hair is rarely seen in Sinai but at least in spring and early summer some extended families live their traditional nomadic way of life. In the mountainous South Sinai, they move to the small villages in the valleys in winter, and in summer they have camps often with stone houses by their orchards in the high valleys.

The tent with the black woven goat-hair roof, the *bayt al-sha'r*, is not only a symbol of North African and Arabian nomads but also an outstanding example of adaptation to the desert environment. The goat-hair shines in the sunlight and reflects the rays. When it rains the hair swells up and becomes watertight. The Bedouin always choose places to erect the tent where it is struck and warmed by the first morning sun, protected from north winds, and shaded by rock walls in the hot afternoon. The tents sides can be opened to let the wind cool the tent. Since in Sinai the tents are very big and heavy, Bedouin do not carry the tents around with them. Frequently a big bundle can be seen hanging in an acacia, and it is unwritten law that no stranger take the bundled tent containing household goods. **(Fig. page 95)**

The conspicuous brushwood huts in North Sinai with their U-shaped ground plan, are also well adapted to desert life. They are always oriented so that the strong and constant northwest winds on the unprotected plain are effectively kept away from the entrance and inner courtyard.

Among other responsibilities, the women have to tend the livestock. A herd of goats accompanied by one or two Bedouin women dressed in black clothes with colorful embroidery, the head covered with a big scarf and the face veiled by a colorful *burqa'* decorated with sequins, coins, pearl buttons, and glass beads are elements typical of Sinai's landscape-a picture already a thing of the past in other areas. The surprisingly husky cries with which the women lead their herds through wadis or the rocky wilderness of the mountains are reminiscent of the harsh cries of big desert birds. In spite of the daytime heat, Bedouin women wear many layers of clothes, which again shows adaptation to the environment. Whereas European women try to wear as few clothes as possible during hot weather, Bedouin women wear many wide skirts on top of each other. The resulting air cushions have nearly the same effect as an air-conditioning system. Covering up also protects against the consequences of ultraviolet rays, hinders too much moisture loss, keeps out dust and wind, and warms in the cold season.

As in other arid zones on earth, the huge herds of goats cause many problems in Sinai. In contrast to sheep, goats nearly wipe out the remaining

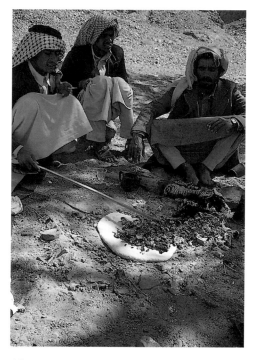

Above:
In the past the small stone mill, the *irha*, was used throughout the Middle East for grinding grain. The grain is poured in through the hole in the middle and the flour falls from the sides onto a cloth spread underneath. The Bedouin bread is baked in the hot ashes of the campfire and tastes delicious when fresh.

vegetation by eating plants down to the roots, thereby contributing to the further expansion of the desert. Even old acacias are not safe from their depredations. If the trunks have grown just slightly slanted, the goats climb the trees to eat every last bit of green. Observations in specially enclosed areas of open desert prove that the natural desert vegetation could be much richer-without goats. When certain species of plants appear plentiful and a very lush green, they are probably poisonous, or at least very bad tasting. Henbane is one such plant.

Date palms are among the most important plants cultivated by the Bedouin. The dates keep well and are highly nutritious, containing plenty of vitamins and minerals. Date palms characterize the landscape of oases and of the Mediterranean coast. Oasis gardens in the north as well as in the high mountain valleys of the south have changed significantly during the last few years. In the past pomegranates, almonds, citrus fruits, olives, figs, carob pods, and sometimes even grapes for wine were the main crops. Today improved varieties of apples, plums, peaches, quinces, and pears are grown to high quality. Along the Mediterranean coast vegetables grow in modern plastic tunnels. Figs and melons grow on sand dunes, while wheat and barley ripen in fields. The farmers no longer reap only for their personal use, but also harvest considerable amounts for the market in Cairo. Cultivation projects in the desert, which seem very successful in the north due to the better water supply, were tried in the south as well, for example in the Qaa Plain north of al-Tur; after a hopeful start, however, these cultivated areas leave only a sad impression.

All the more beautiful appear the old stone-walled orchards in the high mountain valleys around Mount Sinai and Gabal Katrin. Crystal-clear, cool water runs out of fissures and clefts and is conducted to wells and water basins through narrow hoses. Under the fruit trees – and also in the wilderness outside the walls – grows a real herb garden with every possible herb of the East, shaded by huge, gnarled mulberry trees. The Bedouin's knowledge of spices, herbs, teas, and poisonous plants is still part of the traditional basis of their lives. Acacia wood is used for the production of camel saddles, and the bark can be used for tanning skins. In times of need, Bedouin even eat the acacia's resin. By mixing the fruit of a wild caper *(Capparis cartilaginea)* with flour and goat's milk, a cake can be made that will keep for two months. The caper fruits cooked with salt and vegetable oil are a helpful medicine for rheumatism. The tea of the bad-smelling *Cleome droserifolia* helps against chills and against infestation with maggots. Like other peoples living in a natural environment, the Sinai Bedouin have a nearly inexhaustible knowledge of plants and animals in their surroundings.

This knowledge was demonstrated convincingly during a trip of several days through the wonderful high mountain landscape in the area of Gabal Abbas Basha. We found some mulberry trees and ate some of the ripe fruit. It tasted delicious and was refreshing, but its juice covered our hands and clothes with stubborn red stains. For our Bedouin guide this was not a problem. He rubbed some mulberry leaves with water and put the resulting soap-like slime on the red stains, which disappeared immediately.

Bedouin are very superstitious. They told us, for example, the legend of the flying cobra, which attacks people and animals at night and is supposed to be absolutely deadly. Such stories are especially suitable for evenings around the campfire. Incidentally we learned the legend's origin: the famous Greek historian Herodotus reports a strange legend from ancient Egypt, according to which sacred ibises set out every year to fight against poisonous snakes that fly in from a certain wadi. Herodotus even mentions a place near the ancient city of Buto, where he claims to have seen bones of the dead snakes himself.

Bedouin are divided into tribes according to their different origins. It is not easy to give a reliable number of tribes, since whole family clans sometimes split off after quarrels and either join other tribes or become a subgroup of the tribe, or even become a whole new tribe. At present, there exists a kind of confederacy of six tribes in South Sinai with al-Tur as their center. Accordingly they call themselves the Tuwara. All in all, approximately twenty tribes with numerous subgroups exist. Every tribe or group lays claim to a certain area, where it settles or moves around with its livestock. Although the borders are not laid down forever by any means – splits, immigration, and raids have often led to border corrections at least up until the most recent past – it is easy to see that the important territorial borders follow geographical and geological features. Most of these borders are thus natural borders, as is the case for example with the Tih (or Igma) Fault. The location of wells, the course of wadis, and high mountain ridges create natural barriers that Bedouin use to define their tribe's territorial borders. As an exception, we must mention the Gabaliya tribe, whose center even today is St. Catherine's Monastery. On the other hand, the political borders between Egypt and Israel, which have changed again and again in the last decades, never played a role for Bedouin until very recently. Even the MFO (Multinational Force and Observers) Line that was established according to the Camp David Agreement is not accepted by Bedouin today. However, coherent tribal territories now seem to be effectively divided by Egyptian and Israeli border protection for the first time in history. Wandering nomads are a thorn in the side of the military all over the world.

The family is the basic social unit. In accordance with Islamic tradition, a man is allowed to marry up to four women, but the difficult economic living conditions allow most Bedouin to marry only one. A Bedouin from Nuweiba explained that although a young girl is married off by her parents, she is not completely without rights. If she does not like the groom her parents have chosen, she should try to hide from her husband for seven days after he takes her home on the back of a camel (nowadays often by car). If the marriage is not consummated during these seven days, the girl is allowed to return to her parents, and the rejected man is left to the mockery of his friends.

Family life is characterized by a clear division of labor to which every family member makes an important contribution. This situation entails a more independent status for the Bedouin woman than for women in other Islamic societies. Nevertheless, the Bedouin man remains master, which is seen among other things in the way he can much more easily obtain a divorce than a woman can. Men and women each retain the father's name after marriage.

Most of the tasks of a Bedouin woman are related to the tent or house, which certainly arose from the need to care for small children. Apart from running a simple household, women are responsible for small livestock and to turn milk into products that keep, such as sour milk, butter, dry curds,

Bedouin mother and daughter making tea. The woman wears one of the typical hairstyles: the hair is put up like a horn over the forehead, supported inside with a piece of wood or leather.

and cheese. They also weave strips for tents and carpets from goats' hair and sheep's wool and collect wood.

The larger part of the tent is left for the women and children. Strange men are not permitted in this *mahram* ('forbidden') part. An elaborately woven carpet with black and white geometric patterns separates this area from the *sh'ig* part for men. In the latter, male guests meet the host to drink tea. In the women's part of the tent are found the kitchen, a place to store food, and a place for the sleeping-mats of the whole family. The Bedouin still weave on simple looms that are about seventy centimeters wide and are laid out on the ground. Several woven strips are stitched together to produce larger tent walls or roofs.

Usually, young girls or old women keep watch over the small livestock. Since tradition forbids them to ride camels, they always walk. In toughness, stamina, and skills, Bedouin women are equal to men in every way.

The traditional responsibilities of Bedouin men included camel-breeding, leading and protecting their families or clans when moving around from one grazing land to another, defending the tribal territory as warriors, and hunting. In times of need, they also used to raid neighboring tribes or pilgrims on their way to Mecca or trading caravans. Until recently, foreigners were allowed to cross tribal areas only when they rented camels and guides for a fee. At the border the guides would pass the travelers on to the neighboring tribe, which involved having a long tea ceremony and lengthy negotiations. If, as often happened, the neighboring tribes were quarreling, the journey would come to a quick end.

While the women have retained their responsibilities until today and therefore to a large extent their lifestyle, the situation for most men has changed radically. One of the first changes occurred as they became partially sedentary, since animal-breeding and hunting were no longer sufficient to support the family. The pressure to raise crops, like the despised fellaheen, became stronger. Rich Bedouin left – and still gladly leave – this work to poor members of the tribe, giving them a specified share of the harvest in return. When the rich become impoverished, which happens often enough, then they have to plow, carry stones for the fences, and water the orchards themselves.

The already very stressful economic situation of the Bedouin is worsened by the restrictions on their freedom of movement imposed by the military. Since at times their income does not even cover the bare essentials, many Bedouin feel forced to work for a wage in the petroleum fields or in ore mines, at least temporarily.

Once when we searched for a Bedouin guide and camels at the entrance to Wadi Isla for a camel trip to Gabal Umm Shomar, we found only women and children in the small village. All the men were working in al-Tur. Their wives did not know when they would come back. Since Bedouin women are not allowed to ride camels or to guide foreigners, our trip ended here. In the course of the somewhat difficult conversation one woman told us that traditionally the whole clan came together before the men left their families for a time, as a single family is often too small to manage all the work that is necessary to survive in the desert. A larger group, however, is able to manage through cooperation.

Interestingly, tourism combines for some Bedouin new sources of income with old traditions. In some respects, modern camel-tours for tourists revive the ancestral right to lead foreigners through tribal terrritory and to rent camels. At the same time, the increasing contact with foreigners is becoming a problem for the Bedouin. Many men work as gardeners, taxi drivers, tea-sellers, or hotel employees and are thereby confronted with the totally different lifestyle of foreigners who live in modern tourist settlements. Their changed behavior, especially toward strange women, is rather obvious. There is no doubt that Bedouin society has entered a period of radical change since first the Israelis and later the Egyptians began to bring tourists into the area. While Bedouin women and children live their traditional lives in the desert as before, the men vacillate between two contrasting worlds. After several weeks of a fashionable, Western-influenced life, they return to the desert, which is still home to them. The rapid growth of coastal towns like Nuweiba and Dahab shows, however, that the first Bedouin with their whole families are starting to shift the focus of their lives. The temptations of modern life and good sources of income are gradually overcoming ancient traditions.

April 1993: We have established our camp for the night in a wadi not far from the *nawamis*. Lying only in our sleeping-bags on the sand, we wake up several times and watch how the wonderfully clear, starry sky moves above us. The first morning sun has just awakened us when a dignified camel-rider comes from around a bend in the wadi. He immediately takes notice of us and rides toward our camp. *Salam 'alaykum* says the Bedouin, gets off the camel, and starts to take a seat when he notices that we have not yet made a fire to cook tea. He immediately collects some broom twigs, makes an almost smokeless little fire, and puts on the sooty kettle. Only a few minutes later, these tiny burning twigs bring the water to a boil. While the tea steeps, the Bedouin politely waits until we have finished our breakfast, accepting finally only a piece of cake after a threefold invitation. Then, he pours the traditionally very sweet tea and while we all slowly sip the strong hot drink a small conversation starts up. We exchange information about where we come from and where we want to go. While the Bedouin is interested to hear that we are Germans, he tells us that he belongs to the noble tribe of Muzeina, which goes back to one of the seven original Arab tribes. The tethered camel nibbles some herbs in the warming morning sun. After having another glass of tea and a cigarette, the Bedouin stands up, unties the camel and climbs with a last greeting into the saddle. With calm but distance-eating strides, camel and Bedouin amble off between acacias and bizarre sandstone rocks. Again, the early morning stillness becomes almost audible.

Bibliography

Aguilar, J., J. Dommanget, R. Prehac. *A Field Guide to the Dragonflies of Britain, Europe and North Africa.* London, 1986.

Anati, E. *Felskunst im Negev und auf dem Sinai.* Bergisch Gladbach, 1981.

Bemert, G., R. Ormond. *Red Sea Coral Reefs.* Boston, London, 1981.

Cohen, S. *Red Sea Diver's Guide.* Tel Aviv 1978, 1988.

Ditlev, H. A Field *Guide to the Reef-Building Corals of the Indo-Pacific.* Rotterdam, 1980.

Dittrich, P. *Biologie der Sahara.* Ein Führer mit Bestimmungstabellen. Munich, 1983.

Galey, J. *Das Katharinenkloster auf dem Sinai.* Stuttgart, Zurich, 1990.

Gerster, G. *Sinai: Land der Offenbarung.* Berlin, Frankfurt, Vienna, 1961.

Goodman, S. M., P. L. Meininger (eds.). *The Birds of Egypt.* Oxford, 1989.

Hafez, M., H. Marx. *List of Reptiles and Amphibians.* Cairo, 1968.

Heinzel, H., R. Fitter, J. Parslow. *Alle Vögel Europas, Nordafrikas und des Mittleren Ostens.* Hamburg, 1983.

Hobbs, J. J. *Bedouin Life in the Egyptian Wilderness.* Cairo, 1990.

Hollom, Porter, Christensen, Willis. *Birds of the Middle East and North Africa.* London, 1988.

Jahn, W. *"Lebensraum Rotes Meer,"* in *Papyrus* 11, pp.17–20. Cairo, 1989.

Korsching, F. *Beduinen im Negev.* Mainz, 1980.

Larsen, T. B. *The Butterflies of Egypt.* Cairo, 1990.

Lambelet, E. Unpublished sketches and personal communications on the geology and history of Sinai.

Osborn, D. J., I. Helmy. *The Contemporary Land Mammals of Egypt (Sinai).* Chicago, 1980.

Palmer, E. H. *The Desert of Exodus: Journey on Foot in the Wilderness of the Forty Years Wandering.* Cambridge, 1871.

Papyrus *journal with articles on all aspects of life in Egypt* (on Sinai: 2/1987, 11/1989, 11–12/1990, 3–4/1993). Cairo.

Petrie, F. *Researches in Sinai.* London, 1906.

Prinz, O. (ed.). *Itinerarium Egeriae (Peregrination Aetheriae).* 1960.

Randall, J. E. *Red Sea Reef Fishes.* London, 1986.

Rothenberg, B., H. Weyer. *Sinai.* Bern, 1979.

Schiffers, H. (ed.). *Die Sahara und ihre Randgebiete*, vol. 1. Munich, 1971.

Schiller, E. (ed.). *Sinai in Old Engravings and Illustrations.* Jerusalem, 1978.

Schleich, Kästle, Kabisch. *Amphibians and Reptiles of North Africa.* Bonn, 1996.

Schmid, P., D. Pasche. *Unterwasserführer Rotes Meer: Niedere Tiere.* Stuttgart, 1986.

Schmidt, N. *Sinai und Rotes Meer: Reise-Handbuch.* Cologne, 1988.

Schuhmacher, H.. *Korallenriffe: Ihre Verbeitung, Tierwelt und Ökologie.* Munich, Vienna, Zurich, 1982.

Schulz, H.. *"Weißstorchzug: Ökologie, Gefährdung und Schutz des Weißstorch in Afrika und Nahost,"* in *WWF-Umweltforschung* 3. Weikersheim, 1988.

Sharabati, D. *Red Sea Shells.* London, 1984.

Täckholm, V. *Student's Flora of Egypt.* Beirut, 1974.

Tondok, W. u. S. *Ägypten individuell.* Munich, 1991.

Vine, P. *The Red Sea.* London, 1985.

Vine, P. *Red Sea Invertebrates.* London, 1986.

Index (numbers in italics refer to illustrations)